SOME OF DAVID

"After the Bombing"

The True Story of the First African
American HUD/CPD Director
In the State of Oklahoma

ISBN- 978-1-7368699-0-1

Edited and formatted by Shelia E. Bell
www.sheliawritesbooks.com
sheliawritesbooks@yahoo.com

SOME OF DAVID

"After the Bombing"

The True Story of the First African
American HUD/CPD Director
In the State of Oklahoma

DAVID LONG

Table of Contents

Part II – Entering the World of Work

Part III – The Civil Servant Years

Pledge of Obedience

I pledge obedience to myself to make myself a
priority and exercise every effort to be the best I can be.

For those who might not wish me well
(you could kiss yourself and go to…)
I further give myself permission to excel.

No sacrifice or task will be too great or small; it is
my quest to conquer them all. Should I encounter mind
games or make mistakes along the way, I know these
are merely tests to somehow help me win the day.

I might need some learning tools of preparation in
order to be free; this is the only baggage
I want in pursuit of my destiny.

In the end, I refuse to let my *dash* be just another
missed opportunity. My passport is waiting. I can't sit
idly by the fire, if I am to achieve the hopes and dreams
of my heartfelt desires.

Should you fail to digest or not *caught* my drift, my
vision goes far beyond the proverbial cliff.
But please know that it is not my intent to offend
you or burst anyone's bubble.

It's just that I must move on
to overcome my struggles.
I cannot afford to get tired.
I cannot quit.
For it is beyond mediocrity
I have got to git.

There is no temptation,
much less addiction,
to suppress my goal,
but the aforementioned adages
are food for my soul.

Some might call me crazy (horse or dumplings)
and others, perhaps, insane,
but I must apply myself just to stay in the game,
and to reach my highest plane.

Time waits on no one,
and while I'd like to tarry and stay,
excuse my pace as I must be on my bike's way.

Influencers

Walter, Violet and Ermentine Long, Alvin, in particular, and Angelita Watson, Mia Triplett, Aris White, Dr. Robert B. Lyles, Reverend Lee Cooper, Reverend Benjamin Ward, Cecil Harvey, Bishop G. E. Patterson, Aunt Romelia Mason, Mildred Lewis, Alfreda Young, John DeShields, Professor Kumar Jain, R. Buckminster Fuller, Bruce Cook, Hulas King, Alex Little, David Ley; Edgar Woodson, T.C. Warren, Dr. Lemona Evans-Groce, Coretta Scott King, Rosa Parks, Katherine Dunham, President Barack Obama, Senator Everett Dirksen, Secretary Patricia Harris, John H. Johnson, Michael Jordan, John Starks, Curt Flood, Bob Gibson, Tiger Woods, Muhammad Ali, Joe Frazier, Mackler Shepard, Norm Raab, Herb Lowe, Dr. Charles Tollett, Ervin Keith, W.L. Magnus, Harold Jones, George Cooper, Russell Davis, Robert Lerma, and a special thanks to Melvin Long and his wife, Francis; John Pettis, Sr., and Dr. Rodney Coates.

Overview

Dr. Rodney Coates, PhD

"Giving away the government's and taxpayers' dollars has been the easiest part of my job. Finding out what was done with it has proven to be, at times, fairly curious and did not always reflect the desired outcomes in terms of accountability. The ultimate tests have been related to whether or not people have been assisted and their living conditions improved."

David Long is the first and only African American, HUD/CPD Director in the state of Oklahoma, with responsibilities for both the Tulsa and Oklahoma City offices. In Long's tenure with the Department of Housing and Urban Development, in a span encompassing three decades, he awarded in excess of one hundred million dollars to states and local governments for a myriad of community development projects. Without fanfare, he officially retired from his position November 2, 2010.

When David arrived in Oklahoma City in 1995, the downtown area featured only one hotel. The city, in collaboration with David's office, added several others that included the construction of the Renaissance Hotel and the revitalization of the Skirvin Hotel. Other significant partnerships resulted in the Sierra Madre Housing initiative on the south side and the Temple Gardens Senior Citizen Project on the north side, along with the "Gold Dome" (formerly Citizens Bank) at 23rd and Classen Boulevard, in addition to the attraction of the Dell computer facility to the community.

Indeed, Oklahoma City has prospered and moved up on the food chain of cities after David's arrival in 1995, and after the bombing of the A.P. Murrah Federal Building. His charge at that time was to assist HUD in reestablishing its federal presence and facilitate the healing and rebuilding processes within the community.

David's largest single award may have been regarding HUD's Neighborhood Stabilization Program to the State of Oklahoma in an amount approximating 30 million dollars.

Langston University appears to have also benefitted from his advice and guidance, which facilitated their participation in the HUD sponsored HBCU (Historic Black Colleges and Universities) program.

Long's most notable achievements might be related to the St. Louis Metro Area, however, it is Long's belief that the city of Oklahoma is making progress in the areas of economic development, quality of life enhancements and improvements in diversity, through such efforts as the MAPS initiatives.

Long states, "I believe there have been some missed opportunities and that the community has not addressed other compelling challenges. I am a staunch supporter of the stake holding concept and the active involvement of citizens, particularly at the neighborhood level. I do not apologize for my uncommon quest for excellence. Rather, I believe working for the federal government, largest employer in the United States, hiring two percent of the nation's civilian work force, and serving as a civil servant is a noble profession. I further believe my life has been enriched in my endeavors to make a difference in the lives of others." This is his *love* story. This, by the way, is not your typical romantic novel. This is "Some of David."

Expressions from the Author

David Long

After 14 years in Oklahoma City, preceded by 16 years in St. Louis, Missouri and more in the private sector, in addition to service at the local governmental level, now that I am retired, I admit I have yet to have a definitive answer to the *what will I do next* question. When asked what my future plans might entail, I can say I am looking forward to the notion of doing absolutely nothing, which I interpret as the opportunity to do everything.

What better way to honor my retirement and years of service than to tell my story. Thus, "Some of David" was birthed.

"Some of David" entails some of the misadventures I experienced in my role as a mid-level civil servant within the ranks of the Department of Housing and Urban Development (HUD) that embraced the notion of changing the culture of the organization. The efforts and contributions of the change agent were not always appreciated by others who were comfortable in maintaining the status quo in the administration of some of the related projects and programs.

This story includes two other labors of love. The first was seven years as an administrator at the city level. The second labor of love also lasted for seven years as a supervisor of a boys' club. I have over 25 years of trials and tribulations as a civil servant in St. Louis and Oklahoma City.

Often assigned to work in hostile environments, I was reminded that my pigmentation made others uncomfortable. I was informed that I would have to utilize my own coping and survival skills due to the complexities of the organization. Yet, my charge was to assist in changing the culture of the organization.

"Some of David" reveals some of the experiences I was subjected and exposed to from my developmental years through adulthood, along with new skills and abilities, including mother wit that was employed in the process. As "Some of David" unfolds, in my quest for excellence, my values, principles, and mindset are depicted. In light of the presence of racism, the absence of a perfect parental template, the outstanding Black Lives Matter (BLM) issue, and other societal inequities, this portrayal is intended to encourage others, parents in particular, of some expressions of love, advice, and guidance that worked for me. They were beneficial in my upbringing and felt to be applicable to others as a potential resource in light of concurrent and competing issues in today's society. In my view, child rearing can be a complex challenge particularly when exceptions are routinely employed, yet plain and simple as the Ten Commandments.

Part I
The Developmental Years
thru Military

Pre-School

Like any child, I made mistakes and got into mischief. As a preschooler, I was told to stay in the sight of my watchful grandmother. One particular day, she discovered me playing and trying to hide behind some barrels located on the side of her fenced backyard. She picked me up and held me upside down by my ankles and spanked me. Although dangling upside down, I found a railroad spike on the ground. Every time my grandmother struck me, I would strike her leg. The railroad spike was taken from me and presented to my dad upon his arrival from work. The story was told...I was unable to sit down for several days.

On another day, I was cautioned to take care of my brand new jeans while playing in the yard. I climbed on top of a fence to see what was on the other side. In my effort to slide down off the fence, my belt loop became entangled on a nail. When I released my grasp on the top of the fence, I was left in a dangling position unable to reach back and pull myself up. I didn't dare push myself and risk damaging my new jeans.

My grandmother heard my stress filled call for help. She not only lifted me off the fence, she failed to share what happened with anyone.

The Long family resided in a four-unit, cold water flat that featured a common water hydrant on the yard for occupants with two units on ground level and two units upstairs. The ground level units had elevated porches on the backside supported by several strategically located support studs.

Tenants routinely used the space beneath the porch to place their used milk bottles for pick-up by the weekly milkman. I, in my early discovery mode, noticed all of the milk bottles and excitedly ran back into the house and told my mother that I had found the "cow's nest."

I also recalled seeing my dad remove a white insurance salesman from the house. I was quietly playing by myself in the backyard when I looked up and saw my dad holding the back of the insurance man's neck collar, who was in a sitting position, while my dad kicked the salesman's backside all the way down the stairs.

I never learned how or why my dad happened to be home that afternoon and not on his regular job. I listened intently at dinner time for some clarification or acknowledgement of the drama I had witnessed, but none came. Little did I know at the time, but I too would have to just "happen" to be at home when my manhood was being tested. I would be required to define my own set of principles of behavior.

David Long

Off to School

In 1945, at age six, I entered the segregated school system. My walk to school involved passing through the whiskey chute. The whiskey chute was a form of an early *entertainment* district leading to and from the meat packing plants at the lower end of St. Clair Avenue. This strip area consisted of several city blocks and served as the primary corridor with sidewalks only on one side of the street featuring a variety of nightclubs, taverns, juke-joints and a few places to buy ribs and sandwiches. It offered all manner of temptations and diversions for workers at the nearby plants. Paydays and weekends were busy times for this adult entertainment district.

It wasn't uncommon for me to see a wino sweeping out the taverns or removing litter from the parking lots. On occasion, one particular wino would call out with a bit of wise advice, "Hey, stay in school now and don't be like me."

Little did I know, but this unsolicited admonition was being internalized and viewed as being significant and not completely lost upon its recipient, even though, at the time, I did not know why this advice was important. Of course, I graciously accepted my gratuity with a *thank you* as I continued on my way.

On the first day of class, the teacher began the day with a roll-call she read from index cards she had in her hands.

"David Long," the teacher called. "David Long," the teacher called again a second time and then a third time, with no response.

I was sitting on the front row, looking around, saying to myself that this person was absent when the teacher caught my eyes and said, "Hey, you," to which I immediately raised my hand and said, "Here."

On my way home from school one afternoon, my curiosity got me into trouble again. There was a pond of water (Cahokia Creek) not too far from the house that featured a bridge leading into National City called Black Bridge. I felt the need to explore this area, particularly the area beneath the bridge.

I noticed the bridge supports were so close to the edge of the water that I could easily step on the base of the columns supporting the bridge. With the columns being round in shape and with the base being squared up, it left enough room for me to gingerly traverse around the entire column. Of course, I had been warned to avoid this area and of course I did not know how to swim. Somehow, I lost my balance. My feet slipped off of the foundation and I fell, feet first, into the water below. As I disappeared below the surface of the water, I held my breath as my feet touched the bottom of the pond. Intuitively, I bent my knees and pushed myself upwards when my feet touched the bottom of the pond.

I returned to the surface of the water and quickly searched for something to grab hold to. Gasping for air, I sank to the bottom again. The next time I came up I knew I had to grab the base of the foundation from which I had fallen. I managed to do so and carefully maneuvered my body around the platform toward the shoreline to safety.

As I gathered my wits, my larger problem, I concluded, was how I would explain my water soaked condition. I didn't want to explain my circumstance and invite an additional penalty, if not punishment, so I made every effort to remain unseen. I quickly went to the back of the house and found an unlocked window that permitted my re-entry into the house. I changed out of my water soaked clothes and kept silent about my misadventure.

Another mishap occurred after the completion of our summer softball game, the guys were relaxing on the back porch steps reliving the game. I was standing behind one of the guys with a bat in hand, demonstrating my game winning swing as I lined up my bat near the head of my teammate. While demonstrating my swing, I realized that my swing level would not clear the scalp of my teammate - the resulting "thump" and related scream did not go unnoticed. Fortunately, the teammate had a hard head.

One of my best friends and his older brother confronted me about this young lady the brother was smitten by. I attempted to convince them that I had no interest in her but was unable to dissuade them. A fist-fight erupted as both brothers jumped on me. There was no obvious size advantage. My agility and quick hands managed to subdue my attackers in short order as the brothers retreated to their home.

From that moment, I was referred to as "Rooster" after the word got around regarding this incident that was observed by several neighbors. Years later, my brother married this attractive lady and of course the scuffle was soon forgotten, our friendships were renewed and lasted throughout adulthood and the untimely demise of all parties save me and again, well, this was "East Boogie" (East St. Louis's high mortality rate).

A visiting uncle and my dad were sitting on the back porch, sipping beer and chatting while watching me and some of my friends play in the yard. My uncle remarked that he noticed how the kids were enjoying themselves and appeared to perk-up whenever I spoke. He said I might be a leader or something, in addition to possessing a little talent for banter and wit.

Dad's response was that he believed my uncle was only half right, and that I had the potential to become only a half-wit.

Early on, I discovered I liked humor and funny stories which I used at times to turn lemons into lemonade, converting disadvantages into advantages, along with performing my daily chores.

Our back yard became the backdrop and exercise mat for my humorous character trait. Not only did my buddies show up on a daily basis, but my brothers and their friends were also a constant presence.

After completing our chores, we all engaged in activities to the delight of our friends. It didn't take long for me to convince my brothers' buddies to help out with chores so we could have more time for play.

I think it was about the eighth grade when an additional chore was added. My versatility was tested when I was given the responsibility of making breakfast for everyone prior to us going to school. In this regard,

I watched my mother dutifully in advance of my assignment. She would place the skillet on the stove, turn the gas jets on, and add a little cooking oil to the skillet. From there, she would take an egg from the carton, crack it on the top edge of the stove, and drop the contents of the egg into the skillet. *Nothing to it* or so I thought.

On my first day of preparing breakfast, I did everything I believed I saw my mother do. However, I watched in dismay as the egg, which I had mashed too hard, rolled down the front of the stove and never made it into the greased skillet. There was always something else to learn and something else to do. There was never a dull moment in the process of changing from ordinary to extraordinary.

Mom

Violet was my mom's name, and she was pretty as a flower. She was a light-skinned woman with shoulder length hair. Violet was a loving mother to six boys, and a stay-at-home mom. She had managed to complete high school. Dad had to work the fields.

She taught herself how to play the piano via a catalogue she ordered through the mail. Under her supervision, I was assigned to become the new cook in the kitchen.

It was also during this time that I became convinced my parents did not like me. It may have been because I would often ask *why*? Why do we have this or the other when other kids appear to have more freedoms and no chores at all?

Mom said I would understand things as I got older.

It wasn't that my parents did not love their children, because they did. They simply *tailored* their love according to the needs of each child. For instance, if my siblings or I needed attention in certain areas, my parents attempted to fill that need. If you were doing ok, that meant you received less attention. This explanation, however, did not fully convince me that I wasn't being overlooked and not loved by my parents. Little did I know, but I had stumbled upon one of my perceived weaknesses, if not shortcomings. This nuance would surface at inappropriate times and plague me for the rest of my days.

My quiet demeanor was equivalent to the *Silence of the Lamb* overshadowed with sounds of the squeaking "wheels of misfortune" of others. I talked even less when I was only giving instructions.

Mom always said in the absence of anyone loving me...it was paramount that I love myself. Because I loved being around my mother, my brothers said I was a "mama's boy" and her favorite. She taught us to take care of our *temples*, as it is the only body we have. This meant no earrings, tattoos, and definitely no drugs. In spite of my questions regarding life's mysteries, my mom further placed a high regard upon respecting young girls and women.

Dad was not a church-goer, but Mom was a God-fearing woman who required her boys to be regular attendees at Sunday school and church, in general.

The story was told about one of my mom's brothers who was in the military at the time. It was only after his wife, who was very much dark-skinned, arrived at his military duty station did the military realize they had misclassified her husband as white.

Mom's oldest sister was a nurse and the head dietician at a hospital in Winston-Salem, North Carolina. Another brother retired from the Navy. Other members of her family appeared to be successful in their endeavors. Consequently, my brothers and I did not know we were poor and disadvantaged. In our view, we appeared to have as many material things as the other kids in the neighborhood, and Dad kept food on the table.

Mom's lineage is traceable back to the union of the Morrissette and Brazile families, and includes NFL

Hall of Famer, Robert Brazile. I believe I had one of the best moms ever. She was a cheerful giver and provided invaluable advice and guidance. I continue to hold her advice and guidance to my breast in that the principles she taught me have served me well. As she would advise, treat others as you want to be treated. Treat others with love and respect even if you feel that you are dealing with an adversary.

My mother's siblings include her sisters, Romelia, Arlalia, Leitha, Gruenetta and Dothulia, and brothers George, Eural, Charles, and Jonathan. The sisters had a common trait of mutually supporting each other which extended throughout their life spans.

Dad

My dad, Walter, was a handsome, athletic Black man who found employment at a meat-packing plant as an unskilled laborer. He was a self-starter and the forerunner for "Sanford and Son's" junkyard. He saved enough to buy a used truck to support his coal and wood business. My brothers and I were quickly introduced to the art of carrying bushel baskets of coal to his customers.

Dad was not a great communicator, but he never failed to leave chores for all. I was astonished when we watched him add six rooms to an existing three-room house in an area adjacent to East St. Louis referred to as National City, and which became our new residence.

What we did not know was that National City was a company town owned by the vested interests of the stockyards and meat-packing plants within its borders. Viable neighborhoods and related services were not a priority. Indeed, all of the roads were referred to as a plank road.

The area where we lived featured an absence of amenities, i.e. sewer services, parks, fire and police, as well as, mail service. Yet, it was conveniently located within walking distance to Dad's job. Our new home was parallel and adjacent to several railroad tracks leading to the terminal.

One day, by accident, I noticed a pair of binoculars in Dad's lunch pail. My accidental discovery revealed how Dad was able to know exactly what we were doing while he was at work. Looking through his binoculars from the fire escape platform on the side of the building, Dad could observe whether or not we were attending to our chores.

The other lessons taught by my dad involved paying attention to details and staying with a task until it was done. This lesson did not set in immediately, much less the value of hard work and self-discipline. My "Ol' Man" believed idleness was the devil's works. He did whatever it took to discourage us from behaving in mischief.

In spite of the absence of a formal education, one of the items Dad stressed was that we had to learn how to count. He would remain in the truck and tell us how many baskets and how much money we were to collect at each stop. We quickly learned that we never should be short. Dad, sometimes, would take one of us, as a reward, on his trips to the coal mines outside of the city.

I couldn't figure out how my dad managed to track the transgressions of each of his boys. He seemingly would only look and say, "Hey you...that's number one; Hey you...that's number two."

If you reached transgression number three, you were summoned to the "Master's" bedroom. There, you were instructed to drop your pants to your ankles, kneel down, facing him, and place your head between the master's legs as he sat on the edge of the bed. Dad then administered his punishment (beat your ass) typically with a leather belt. This would continue until he was satisfied that the penalty was equal to your mistakes or until he got tired. Like me, I was sure my other brothers had cried and kicked to extricate themselves from Dad's knees, but to no avail or unable to do so.

Needless to say, it only took one or two trips to the master's bedroom before you determined that you should be a model young boy and conduct yourself accordingly, as they would tell us in Sunday School.

Dad was a man's man in that other men in the neighborhood frequently sought his counsel. I don't know to this day how he mastered certain skills to the extent he was viewed by his peers as a jack-of-all-trades in spite of his limitations in a formal sense and his disinterest in communicating to others who or where he had accumulated the universe of information he possessed, save through the school of hard knocks, it was presumed.

Walter's siblings include brothers Leroy and Thomas, and sisters Irene, Cora, Lela Bell, Clara, and Savanah.

Early Days

Garfield (first thru fourth) and Carver (fifth thru eighth) served as the grade schools for the northeastern part of East St. Louis, Illinois. Commonly referred to as "Goose Hill," this all-Black area of the city consisted of small neighborhoods with several commercial outlets consisting of hardware stores, grocery stores, a pharmacy, a meat packing plant, and a grain weight station.

On the walk to school, it wasn't uncommon for the yellow school bus, carrying white kids, who lived further away, to get caught in traffic. The bus full of kids only moved a little faster than the kids who were walking. On several occasions white kids on the bus would call us out of our names (.i.e. there goes a *chocolate*, there goes a *vanilla*). Little did I know that the racial overtones and historical inequities would remain outstanding and seemingly irresolvable.

On another occasion, I repaired my first flat on my bicycle. The bicycle was the result of finding a discarded bike that entailed other repair needs. After saving a few pennies, I was able to buy a tire repair kit to patch the inner tube and re-insert it into the rubber tire itself. I was quietly proud of myself for my accomplishment without assistance from anyone. After fixing the flat, I took the bike to the neighborhood filling station to put air into the repaired tire.

In the process of filling the tire with air, I noticed a large sign with the words FREE AIR. I decided to take full advantage of the free air by getting as much as I could. The repaired tire blew-up in my face. I hoped I had enough materials left over to fix the tire again. Walking the bike home, I told myself from now on to be very cautious of *free things*.

Saturday nights involved taking a full bath, no matter the season or the time of year. Our house featured coal-burning stoves. There were two tubs placed near the stove full of heated water.

On one particular evening, I was taking my bath, when something distracted me. Suddenly, my rear end made contact with the hot stove. I knew immediately that I had a new problem and a new birthmark.

Often, I watched my mother wash our clothes. When charged to do so, I attempted to repeat her actions. She would remove a few items of clothing from around the agitator and then line them up in order to feed them through an attached ringer on top of the machine. I did not know that I needed to pull my fingers back from the ringer rollers—not until it was too late. The ringer continued to spin and turn as it pulled my arm up to my elbow. At the eleventh moment, I found the release button for the ringer and was able to remove my arm. I was too embarrassed to tell my mom or anyone about the incident.

I made another mistake regarding the stove. When told to re-start the fire one morning, I attempted to bypass the normal start up and instead I doused kerosene on top of the old bed of coals, struck a match, and threw the match onto the waiting kerosene. The blast from the ignited liquid burned off my eyebrows and left more than embarrassment upon my face.

There were seemingly endless chores dispensed by my dad. One summer project would involve digging a trench for a new water line. Initially, I embraced the project since it meant we would have the benefit of indoor plumbing.

Dad outlined the specifications in great detail. He purchased special tools for this activity which included a pick, a shovel designed for this type of job, string, and measuring rod sets. The difficulty of this task was related to the nature of the soil, perhaps the earlier river bottom that was akin to concrete as we took turns carefully following his instructions.

Devoting no less than four hours per day throughout this one summer, my brothers and I were finally able to inform our dad of its completion. Our joy was quickly extinguished when Dad told us he did not have the money to buy the pipes and we would have to refill the trench. I was so upset, although I could not openly express it.

My dad's teaching of staying with a task until it was done did not set in immediately, much less the value of hard work and discipline. Daddy believed idleness was the devil's workshop, and he did what he did to discourage mischief.

Our Games

Approaching eighth grade, one of the things I enjoyed doing was playing basketball. Not having a basketball of my own made me dependent upon friends to use their ball, something I did not like.

Leading up to Christmas, I sounded like a broken record. I constantly told my parents, but especially my mother, "All I want for Christmas is a brand new basketball."

Finally, Christmas Day arrived. I was the first of my brothers to surround the Christmas tree, looking for a square box reflecting my only wish. My search came up with me being empty handed. I was devastated.

Mom said there was a special gift for me. She presented me with a pencil and pen set.

My friends and I engaged in a variety of games, particularly softball, football, and stickball. We also created our own games to entertain ourselves. Playing Cowboys and Indians involved pulling up a tall sunflower plant and placing a shoelace behind the head of our horse with the flowered blooms sweeping the sidewalks behind us. We compressed pet milk cans on the bottoms of our shoes to imitate the sound of the hoofs of galloping ponies.

The next level of our cowboy playing involved having a shoot-out. Instead of using our cap and pistols, we thought a BB gun would make it more fun. This was quickly discouraged by the parents after one of their sons returned home with an unexplained "mask" on his forehead.

Building my own roller-derby racer became a major project in terms of finding and assembling the items and materials needed for this activity. Also, none of my friends ever revealed the visitations, after closure of the nearby barns, for the purpose of riding the real horses that were kept there for short periods of time. As it is said, there was seldom a dull moment.

Larry Darnell

My parents, Walter and Violet Long had six boys—Walter George, David Harold (Me), Melvin James, Charles Douglas, Albert Lester, and Larry Darnell.

Larry Darnell, the youngest of my brothers, was born with a deformity commonly referred to as "waterhead baby." According to the doctor, my brother's condition, which is medically known as hydrocephalus, would result in a short life-span of perhaps six years.

When word of this circulated among the neighboring kids, many wanted to see this *unusual* abnormality.

Our parents determined that Larry would be loved and treated no differently than the rest of us. My brothers and I believed Larry was special. We resolved to protect him.

Other than his physical deformity, Larry was normal, requiring no special accommodations. He learned how to balance himself and accomplished all the things other babies and young boys accomplished.

Dad created a semi-private courtyard area with a paved circular walk and a small flower garden in the middle where Larry could ride his tricycle.

Larry had reached and passed his fifth birthday. On this particularly warm afternoon, I was watching him ride his tricycle. It was noticeable that he was sweating profusely. Larry suddenly stopped his tricycle in front of the flower garden, got off his tricycle, and began to pull weeds from around the flowers.

20

I observed how carefully Larry balanced himself while meticulously removing the weeds. I asked him what he thought he was doing. He said, "I want to show my father what a good worker I am."

I was startled and confused because the word "father" was never used in our household. We always called our daddy, "Daddy." When I told my mom about what Larry did and said, she quickly held Larry tightly to her breast.

Later that summer, Larry passed away in his sleep. Little did I know, as the second son, I was the 'pick of the litter' and would become the only college graduate.

Mom's Struggles

Mom called an uncommon meeting one late summer afternoon. Without providing much detail, she announced that she was frustrated, exhausted and had reached her limits with Dad. After much consternation and thought, she told us she was leaving, and that we, the three oldest boys, had the option of leaving with her or remaining at home with our dad.

We were not told what the immediate plan was as she awaited our response. As I searched for some solutions regarding mom's complaints and the unknowns associated with her departure plans, my brothers quickly indicated that they would support her decision and would leave with her. I, then, realized that all eyes were on me as I remained silent in processing my mom's concerns.

I quietly indicated that in light of their determination, someone needed to stay behind and protect the home and therefore, I would remain. Mom and my brothers packed a few items in various bags and departed without telling me where they were going.

When Dad arrived home later that day, I informed him of the circumstances as I understood them. Dad listened intently without comment. He gave me a look that said not only was he shocked at this development but would have never guessed that "Mama's Boy" had remained and not left with the rest.

Two weeks after leaving, my mom and brothers returned. It was business as usual upon their return, with no further discussions or follow-up. This was the little that I knew or was not told.

An Addition to the Family

There would be another incident that surfaced not long after Mom returned home. It was announced by my mother that my brothers and I had an older sister who lived in Tupelo, Mississippi.

As we looked among ourselves, the silence was soon broken when I blurted excitedly, "Where did you say our sister was? We need her here with us so she can help us with housework."

The other brothers quickly joined in with similar responses. In light of this chorus of interest, and overall response, Dad said they were putting together a plan for all of us to go to Mississippi to meet her. This outing would also permit Mom to reconnect with this daughter that had never been mentioned or called to our attention before.

There were never any adverse concerns expressed regarding whatever the circumstances might have been surrounding our mysterious sister. In retrospect, we were too young and naive to envision any prior indiscretions regarding this development. Somehow, I knew not to ask my mom if this info might be related to her discontent. My sister remains a precious gift and viable sibling who I continue to talk to on a regular basis.

Middle School

My middle school years (5th through 8th) at Carver High School, featured an outstanding principal and committed Black teachers. Most of us (students) were unaware that the city and school district recognized the inevitable integration of schools, which they determined would occur at the ninth grade level. This decision took place in the early 50's, prior to *Brown-vs-the Board of Education,* Topeka, Kansas in 1954.

The parents of the students were not privy to all of the special efforts undertaken to prepare their kids for the merger of divergent cultures at this grade level. No one knew in advance what the consequences would be. The teachers took a personal interest in each student and presented lesson plans beyond the eighth grade. The reactions to these efforts were not always positive. Monthly PTA meetings were well attended with a litany of complaints regarding discipline and homework assignments.

I recall a visitation by the mother of one of the students, with a butcher knife in hand, attempting to assault a teacher for spanking her child. On a separate occasion, at the close of a PTA meeting, a teacher fled on foot after being confronted by unknown parties, which resulted in him leaving his vehicle parked in front of the school. Some of the other students, hearing of this incident, were impressed by the swiftness and overall speed of the fleeing teacher as he outran his pursuers. No one ever explained why the principal was permitted to drive around with a sawed-off shotgun prominently mounted on the dashboard of his car.

9th Grade

Rock Junior High could be described as a castle-like stone building. It was within walking distance of my home—a long walking distance.

At school, I learned I needed a lock and key for my assigned school locker. This was unfamiliar to me as there were no locks or keys on the home front, and no one locked their homes. I further discovered that classroom seats were assigned alphabetically, meaning I would not be able to sit in the front-row seats.

Another discovery occurred when I was asked to read the information written on the blackboard. "What blackboard?" I had asked.

When I arrived home from school that afternoon, I quickly told my mom about the blackboard incident. Shortly after, I was tested and outfitted with glasses for the first time in my life. I was thirteen years old.

Many other students at Rock Junior High appeared to be from places I had only read about in geography. There were boys and girls of European descent and from countries such as Lithuania, Czech Republic, Germany and Poland, among other Caucasians within the student body. I surmised that I, and the limited number of other Black students, would be in the minority, in addition to noting that there were no Black teachers.

Boys and girls were given separate homeroom assignments and went to certain classrooms, according to our class schedules. My homeroom teacher worked at a mortuary in addition to his teaching job. Sometimes he told us intriguing and humorous stories about his experiences.

I involved myself in a number of school activities, including going out for the track team. After practice, I would return to the gym and shower before leaving for home. I noticed that many of my peers had underarm hair and chest hair. The unanticipated consequences of having been placed in a higher grade began to sink into my mental processes. Considering my options as compared to the majority of my peers, I decided to focus on academics as opposed to track and field.

I further embraced my new school environment by announcing my candidacy for president of my class. With a newly found white classmate, I orchestrated a colorful campaign.

I did not win, but at least the other students became aware of who I was as did my community. My efforts were also rewarded with a set of encyclopedias from my aunt in North Carolina. An article appeared in *The Crusader* (the local newspaper) at the end of the school year. *See newspaper clipping below.*

A DESERVING HONOR

It is no secret why the Walter Longs, Sr. are wearing a happy smile these days. Their son, David, tried to win all the honors at Rock Jr. High. Along with his certificate of promotion to the Senior High School he received the American Legion School Award Certificate of Honorable Mention. Students and teachers vote for recipients. Outstanding scholarship and achievement are required for runner-up in the American Legion School Award Program; and recognition is also given to the accomplishment and the development of the qualities of honor, courage, leadership and service. The award was made by Post No. 53, the Department of Illinois.

David also received two Rock Jr. High School Certificates of Merit for superior achievement in Algebra and in General Science. Most outstandng of all, he earned a membershp in the National Junior Honor Society of Secondary Schools.

High School

My high school years went swiftly. The Black students appeared to be tolerated, if not otherwise ignored. Exceptions were made for the ones who excelled in sports.

There were only a few Black teachers. I was encouraged by the white teachers to take shop and woodworking classes as opposed to math, science and Latin I had signed up for. When the results of the school's SAT scores came out, several of the teachers accosted me and asked if I was David Long when they saw my high SAT scores.

I do not recall any comments or references to the availability of counseling or scholarship opportunities. At the student assembly prior to our formal graduation ceremonies, I was surprised at the announcements regarding scholarships, although several Black athletes received offers in their sports area.

Other barriers were quietly being removed. The excursion steamboat (Admiral) was the site for our high school prom. It made an exception regarding their normal practice of exclusion and allowed the Black students to attend the prom. I made my presence known by inadvertently wondering into the ladies' lounge during the excursion. The female classmates were not amused.

During summer break, an unexpected opportunity occurred. Mom's youngest sister and her policeman husband needed babysitting help. At the time, they were living in the basement of the new home they were building. Their home was located in an area across town and down the street from a funeral home and the Myles Davis residence.

In my view, their need of a babysitter permitted me with a legitimate opportunity to avoid the burdensome daily chores around the house and put a modest few dollars in my pockets.

I did not fully understand what I had committed myself to regarding my babysitting chores. The youngsters were forever getting into something, and required my full attention in my new role and related supervisory responsibilities.

I also did not anticipate the ongoing construction of the house. I became the gopher and learned some of the basics of construction, like carpentry, various types of saws, and even brick-laying.

By my senior year, my uncle, with help from others, completed the house and adjoining garage. Family members were invited to celebrate the occasion. It can be noted that I never elected to share my summer experiences with my schoolmates or teachers.

This Is It

Having graduated at 17 with the January class of 1957, I did not have a care in the world. I had given little thought of what I might do beyond high school and instead I welcomed the ridiculous notion of doing absolutely nothing.

My daydreaming was immediately shattered when my dad advised me that he needed to meet with me in his office. I asked myself what sin of commission I could be guilty of. This uncommon demand became even more confusing when I realized I did not know where my dad's office was located.

I watched my dad remove himself from the kitchen table. He retreated to the back porch and proceeded into the backyard. From there, he walked through the gate to an inclined pathway leading away from the house.

I dutifully followed behind him.

He turned mid-way up the incline and looked down on me and said, "This is it."

I wasn't sure if my dad meant that this space was his office or if he was talking about something else.

Dad proceeded to help me by informing me that he and my mother had talked. The results of the talk revealed that he and my mother had determined that there was little else they could do for me. They both felt that I had done well in school; however, my attainments did not change the reality that they simply did not have any money to further my education.

Dad then told me there was a big world waiting for me. He wanted me to know that they felt I had the talent to do whatever I chose to do. Dad added that there were a lot of good women out there in the world and that I might want to find me one.

He paused long enough for me to raise one of many unanswered questions.

"What's a good woman?" I asked.

Dad gazed at me and announced, "The meeting's over." He turned away and returned to the house.

I began to process the information and implications of the summit meeting with my dad. The ominous nature and related unknowns were unsettling and problematic. I tried to understand my dad's point of view. I surmised, Dad was trying to delicately inform me that my non-contribution to the overall expenses related to his parental responsibilities was in need of adjustment. After all, I was residing under his roof and consuming his food, while doing or offering nothing in return.

I must admit that I had failed to think what I would do beyond 12th grade. Did the world really owe me something or was I really entitled to something that I had not earned? *How could I make withdrawals from the bank when I had not made any deposits into the account?* I asked myself. I further reminded myself of a missed opportunity with my aunt in Winston-Salem, North Carolina. She had offered to underwrite my educational expenses and provide lodging if I would join her household and attend one of several Black colleges that were not far from her residence.

One of the few things I knew was that I could not see myself being a teacher. This was why I had declined her offer, much less, trying to figure out how I would repay her generosity. I then decided I would get a job.

Job Search

I started my job search by obtaining a copy of the local newspaper and going through the want-ads section. I shared my objective with my pastor and a few politicians and obtained their permission to cite them as character references.

I visited several places in the metropolitan area, took numerous tests, and even obtained a few interviews, but no job offers.

Finally, one interviewer asked me to stay after the dismissal of other candidates. He told me he had been impressed with my test scores, and wanted me to know I had done exceptionally well on the entry level exam. He then added that in spite of passing the exam, they would not offer me a job because of the ongoing military draft.

That was when I realized there was something else I did not know. The interviewer explained that due to me being underage that employers would be required to make certain commitments regarding any employees who might be summoned by the military. As a consequence, their policy was not to hire anyone who had not registered with the draft board or satisfied any related obligations.

On my way back home, it dawned on me that there were no references/discussions concerning the draft at home nor in school. Additionally there was no acknowledgement of the disappearance of my older brother to the Marine Corps several years earlier.

The Military

Shortly after the interview, I determined that a similar exit such as the one my older brother made to join the Marine Corps, might be necessary. I would need my parent's signatures to enlist.

The recruiting offices were located in a federal building in the downtown area of St. Louis. I visited several offices where their processing procedures and programs were explained. Interviews, tests, and medical exams were identified as preliminary steps prior to signing up for any of the military opportunities.

After testing with the Army, Navy, and Marine Corps, I was advised that I did well on all of the testing and could select any branch of service. Each recruiter emphasized the potential benefits their specific service could provide.

I settled on joining the U.S. Marine Corps. The recruiter told me they would provide a commitment wherein I would receive training to become an airplane pilot. Armed with this information, I proudly presented this novel opportunity to my parents and requested their signatures in support of this offer.

Mom and Dad gave me their blessings and signatures that resulted in me being enrolled and processed into the Marine Corps by the end of February.

The first stop on my journey into the military world was San Diego, California for boot camp. Before I officially left the household, my undeveloped maturity and naivety caused me to say something I later regretted. My dad and I were looking for something in their closet, which was dominated with my mother's garments and imitation mink coat.

Without thinking, I commented, "You mean to tell me that after all of these years you only have one pair of pants, one shirt, and two ties? That won't be me." Dad's face fell in disappointment.

"I refuse to defend my choices, but you just keep living," Dad told me.

Without fanfare, my parents delivered me to Union Station, the train depot in St. Louis. The scenic, two-day trip was uneventful. Upon arrival, a chartered bus took us to a large parking area in front of a fenced in facility identified as Camp Pendleton.

When the bus driver opened the doors, we were immediately confronted by a uniformed Marine who directed us to get off the bus, line up, and get down and perform ten push-ups.

I was wearing my Sunday pants and dress shoes. It had rained earlier so there was a standing puddle of water on the asphalt parking lot.

In spite of my concern of getting my dress shoes soaked, the Marine screamed, "That means you! Now get down and give me ten!"

Little did I know that this was the beginning of a hellish four month training cycle that would test and strain my physical and psychological capacities. We were told we would be sequestered without any contacts beyond camp itself. There would be no radios, TV, or newspapers allowed. Any and all correspondence for recruits would be screened before mailing. We were only to tell our loved ones that we were having a good time.

These pronouncements sent shockwaves throughout the new recruits as we feared other unknown commands and demands. The Marine instructors, it was declared, would be our new parents and give us everything we might need. I surmised that this might not be the typical summer camp, after all. My premonitions were quickly realized when we (the recruits) were unceremoniously baptized into the regimen of boot camp training.

The barracks were barnlike looking structures that would serve as our new homes. Each recruit was assigned a bunker and a wooden foot locker for our belongings. There was a separate restroom hut nearby. The drill instructors were housed among the huts, all neatly lined up in rows.

The sound of the bugle aroused us in the a.m. and TAPS signaled the close of the day.

Getting dressed, we visited the restroom next door for shaving and grooming before marching to the mess hall for breakfast, after which the fun would begin.

We marched everywhere...to the athletic field for exercises, followed by running around the track with our backpack on and carrying our M-1 rifle. Recruits were expected to swim across the swimming pool and climb up several diving platforms and then dive into the pool. Some recruits were assisted along by instructors with cattle prods and boxing gloves attached as recruits screamed on their way into the pool.

There were classroom sessions held on various military equipment, the M-1 rifle, and regular trips to the firing range to practice shooting from different positions. The monotony of these activities could be suffocating and often unrelenting. We did get a day of rest on Sunday. My salvation rested on the notion that if they killed me, I would be of no benefit to anyone, including the Marines. In addition, my G.A. (God, my guardian angel) would not permit/tolerate my death as an acceptable outcome. The art of digging a foxhole, in addition to refilling it, does not invite any pleasant memories.

Post Boot Camp

After the four month indoctrination period came to an end, I was back on the train for the two day and one night trip to St. Louis. My window seat allowed me an opportunity to absorb the scenic collage of colors and the ever changing landscape. The clatter of the wheels was music to my ears and lulled me into thoughts of my transformation. I had managed to survive the ordeal of this almost indescribable experience.

The training itself encompassed all of the ingredients deemed necessary as a precursor to wearing the uniform that adorned me, and reflected several merit badges including one for my rifle marksmanship. All were penned on my proud chest. Approving glances acknowledged my presence. *Wow!* I was finally recognized as being somebody.

As the discomfort of the window seat began to sink in, I was reminded of the embarrassment I felt regarding several Black recruits who were given sticks and stones to be held in their hands because they did not know their right hands from their left hands.

I also felt sorry for the recruit who failed to bathe properly, and was subjected to a steel-brush washing of his naked body by other recruits under the direction of the drill instructor.

I also thought about the recruit who apparently slipped and hung himself on the fence surrounding the base in an effort to escape the camp.

I smiled when I recounted the drill instructor's challenge to fight any recruit on a one-on-one basis, if we had the nerve to take him on. About ten of us recruits responded to the challenge. The instructor then surprised us with the announcement that each of us who had accepted the challenge would become a squad leader. The boxing matches never occurred.

Notwithstanding the rigors of the daily marching drills, I reflected on the classroom counseling sessions that involved a wide range of subjects. They regularly included race relations. They had in-place a no tolerance policy regarding racial matters. We had to be our brother's keeper.

It surprised me how the instructors bluntly attacked racial inequalities and debunked all preferential theories, as a result of one's birth. The discussions of inalienable and constitutional rights, and the treatment of other indelicate notions, so upset the conscience of one white recruit, that he blurted out that he would not return to his hometown. He added that his parents and ministers had not only deceived him, but they had lied to him as well. He now knew that Black guys really did not have tails.

Finally, the train ride made its arrival back to Union Station. I quickly grabbed my bag of belongings and eagerly awaited my departure from the train. I saw my parents among the crowd of people meeting the train.

I heard my dad shout, "Boy, are we glad to see you. When are you leaving?"

I almost did a turn-about as I tried to digest this mixed and confusing statement. I stepped off the train and hugged my mom. For a few days, I enjoyed visiting my family and a few relatives before I boarded another train destined for Jacksonville, Florida. Little did I know of the surprise that awaited me there.

Naval Training Centers

At the Jacksonville Naval Training Center, I was processed for the aircraft training program. My introduction included welcoming remarks from the trainers. They provided an orientation and overview of the anticipated training, along with information regarding amenities such as food, lodging, and a class picture taken of all new trainees.

Everything appeared to be going smoothly. I immersed myself into my field of studies and my new environment. After several weeks of classwork, we were exposed to various shops, hangars, and airplanes.

Cockpit training involved learning the dashboard of instrument panels and how to read them. This included the start-up and stopping procedures, all under the supervision of staff trainers. One particular afternoon, I climbed up the ladder and was settled in the cockpit. Practicing the assigned procedures, the supervisor on the ground signaled for me to cut the engine off and come down from the trainer plane.

Little did I know that my dreams of following in the steps of the Tuskegee Airmen would be shot down by this supervisor. The distressed instructor looked at me and asked me if I always wore my glasses, and I told him I did.

The instructor informed me that the Marine Corps pilots were required to have 20/20 vision. He couldn't explain how I managed to get this far in their program without my corrective lenses being noted. He was sure, under the circumstances, I would be unable to become a pilot. He told me to stand-by until they sorted the matter out.

The following day, I was ushered into the instructor's office for an unscheduled meeting attended by other Marine Corps personnel representatives. They identified several options and alternatives that could be considered:

1. Reassignment to the School for Navigators
2. Assignment to the Officers' Cadet Program to become a commissioned officer with the provision that I extend my military service for an additional two years
3. Selection of another field of training of my choosing
4. A honorable discharge without prejudice

They acknowledged the commitment of pilot training plainly evident in my personnel folder, but no apology was offered. I was advised that I would have a short time to inform them of my determination after spending only six-weeks at the naval training center.

I, unemotionally, examined my options and developed a matrix of pros and cons regarding each option. I had no mentors or guidance counselors that could help me. Yet, clinging to my interest in the field of aviation, I recalled a major aircraft manufacturer (McDonnell Douglas) located in St. Louis. I thought I might get a job there after the completion of my military obligations. This was subsequently agreed upon. Arrangements were made for me to attend an electronics school at a naval center in Memphis, Tennessee.

The training center was located just outside of Memphis in Millington, Tennessee. Its mission was to serve as an aviation and pilot training center for personnel in the Navy as well as the Marine Corps.

For the next six months, I was exposed to an intensive electronics and maintenance regimen. Instructions were provided in a classroom setting on a daily basis with weekends off.

Off the base I was introduced to southern hospitality that I was unfamiliar with in the form of segregated practices and Jim Crow laws, in addition to second class citizenship in spite of my uniform.

Upon leaving the base, we were reminded by the bus driver that we were to take the seats at the back of the bus and to behave ourselves in town.

In Memphis, I noticed the *black and white* water fountains; was introduced to the balcony area of the movie (after entering the movie through the emergency exit on the side of the building in order to get to the spiral staircase leading up to the balcony), and learned that Blacks could visit city owned parks on the last Wednesday of each month, among other restrictions.

In spite of the prevailing policies (1958), I found Memphis to be a welcomed change of pace to the rigors of daily training and a popular place to visit that featured a variety of interest points that included Beale Street, Sun Records Recording Studio, home of Elvis and other lesser known blues musicians. Also, Memphis was only an estimated 300 miles south of St. Louis which afforded me an opportunity to go back home over holiday weekends. It was when we reached the half-way point to Sikeston, Missouri that the bus driver would announce that we, the blacks, could sit anywhere on the bus.

After completing the intense electronics program in Memphis, I had to report to a Marine Corps air base located in Iwakuni, Japan, where I remained for approximately one and a half years. Not only was the country foreign to me, everything was foreign. I was entering a whole new world.

The New World

The base in Iwakuni, Japan featured jet fighters and large cargo planes but no electronics shop for the gauges, devices, and instruments that I had been trained to repair. I was ultimately assigned to the staff that supported airport operations. This involved working on flight lines, directing planes to various hangars, driving mobile generators and hooking them up to start the planes for the pilots. I became a member of the flight crews for the large transport planes delivering supplies to bases located throughout the Far East.

Orientation and introductions included an assessment of skills wherein I received temporary assignments to the administrative office, as well as serving as a military police officer (MP) responsible for the security of the base and related matters.

As a military police officer, I was exposed to the misadventures and misdeeds of my fellow servicemen. My typed reports were labeled classified and discreetly filed away. I was required to swear not to reveal this classified information to anyone. The reality was that the most egregious violations were routinely swept under the proverbial rug.

These assignments invited the rapid assimilation and growth in divergent areas previously unknown to me. My values and sensibilities were routinely tested as I noted the disparate treatment accorded a defeated country and its people, as well as the biased news reporting of the American occupation for the press releases back home. I took no solace in visiting the memorable sites in Hiroshima and Nagasaki that revealed the horrific effects of war.

The museums presented, in graphic details, the impact of the atomic bomb upon these cities. While I had heard about World War 2, there were no words in my vocabulary to describe, process, or even digest what I saw. For instance, I saw this fruit-sized jar containing a liquid substance and what appeared to have been a bicycle. The bicycle had been reduced to the size of earrings. At the end of the tour, there was a sobering admonition that this type of holocaust should never be unleashed again upon any other country, anywhere in the world.

I had great difficulty recording the interview of a Japanese *lady of the evening's* sexual account with a commissioned officer who had a heart attack and died during the encounter. His erect penis had to be broken prior to shipping his remains stateside. A medal of merit commemorating the deceased officer's outstanding service to his country would accompany his remains to the family. A related report of his valiant and meritorious conduct in a military action with undisclosed persons could not be revealed. I was relieved when I learned that I would be reporting to the airport support unit shortly.

This was an important lesson in that I had not been cleared via the security clearance process, nor did my grade level accord me access to personnel information of the nature I stumbled upon. Consequently, my temporary administrative support was terminated shortly thereafter, which met with my silent approval.

The local people were subjugated and relegated to a rank of inferiority. Reports on the native people, including the selling of their children, were not uncommon in their desperation and efforts to survive.

These factors contributed to a maturation process leading to a new reality for me. I attempted to assuage my conscience by persuading my newly found Puerto Rican buddy (Vasquez) to try out for the high-speed softball team, champions of all of the other military teams based in the Far East. I further took language and Judo classes. I was quickly advised that this all white team featured returning veterans at all positions, and it would be an exercise of futility to even participate in the trials for the team. The speed and youthful exuberance of my buddy and I prevailed when we were added to the team as back-ups.

The exchange rate (360:1) resulted in the view that my money was like play money. I was able to buy all types of souvenirs from off-based vendors. Quality suits and custom made shirts were among the many items I shipped home.

The Japanese culture featured an anomaly wherein the Japanese wife was to be subservient to her mate. She should always sit on a stool lower than her husband; only walk behind him, and never alongside him. The primary purpose of the female was to serve her husband. As a result, a number of interracial marriages occurred, particularly involving Black servicemen.

I recalled the summit meeting with my dad and the suggestion that I might want to find myself a good woman. It appeared that a Japanese woman might be one of the better choices. I listened to the various debates on this subject. In spite of all the benefits stated, I felt it was not the time for me to make such a life altering decision.

I am also reminded of an incident involving one of my teammates who appeared to have picked up something he did not need, but he did not want to visit the Health Unit on base for fear of his visit becoming known by other teammates, which might compromise his position as a starting player. A plan was carefully crafted involving a visit to the office of an English speaking Japanese doctor and we discreetly found our way to the doctor's office.

Upon our entry, the doctor stood up, bowed and said, "Hi, how are you?"

My buddy was so relieved that he bubbled over in his explanation of his health concern. The doctor listened politely. When the explanation was complete, the doctor bowed his head again and said, "Hi, how are you?"

♣

My rank had reached the Corporal E-4 level, which is equivalent to sergeant. An injury afforded me an opportunity to be in the starting line-up at the shortstop position even though I was relegated to batting ninth in the batting order.

My stellar play on defense and timely hitting on offense frequently resulted in me being cited as the star of the game. The star of the game would be treated to a short ride with the base commander in his jet plane.

An exuberant fighter pilot was grounded after he buzzed a local beach. His punishment was the assignment as the overall manager of the team. His first move involved changing the batting order. I learned that I would be batting from the clean-up spot, the 4th position rather than the 9th. In spite of my bespectacled facade and slim appearance, I continued to excel with a batting average in excess of 400 for the remainder of the season. It could also be noted that the team won the championship again. I was able to keep my spikes and glove at the end of the season.

This further meant the loss of the care-free benefits that all of the players were accorded. That included not having to perform their regularly assigned duties. I was returned to the support unit and the routines related to flight operations. I regained my status as a crew member involving flights to Korea and related bases throughout the Far Eastern Zone.

However, this dynamic period of developments was rapidly coming to a close. In the waiting area I overheard whispers and rumors concerning several who could not be accounted for. I thought about the classified reports I had previously typed and this circumstance would be described as MIAs (serviceman missing in action)

We soon boarded the USNS Gaffey at Yokosuka for the return to the mainland. I had learned much about myself and the exposed realities and indiscriminate behavior of my fellow countrymen. I knew I would continue to digest both cultures—Japan and the military—as they would leave indelible impressions. I further ingested the brief stopovers in Guam, Hawaii and my subsequent disembarkment at San Francisco, California.

The Short Timer

The elongated travel time back to the States afforded me the opportunity to reaffirm my value system, articulate my philosophy of life, along with my goals and objectives once discharged. Discussions with other returnees revealed a number of plans, including one Marine who desired to be a blackjack dealer in Las Vegas, of all things.

My immediate travel orders identified a Marine Corps base located in Beaufort, South Carolina as my next duty station. I had reviewed my earlier commitment to send money home through an allotment entrusted to my Mom. I also learned about another benefit referenced as the G.I. Bill that would be available to me in executing my game plan.

Upon my arrival and settlement, I was issued an M-1 rifle typically reserved for Marines assigned to the infantry component of the Marines. I was surprised at the jealous reception accorded me as a young 20-year old CPL-E4. With only a few months to go, and light duties being assigned, a career sergeant informed me that he was a recruiting officer and since the farm crops were in great distress that I should immediately reenlist. I informed the sergeant that he was doing himself a disservice wherein he had failed to review my personnel folder, which indicated my originating entry point as the city of St. Louis. Consequently, I had no frame of reference for farming matters called to my attention by the sergeant. Nonetheless, the Christmas holidays were around the corner. I made plans to visit my aunt in Winston-Salem for that extended weekend. The saga with the sergeant was yet outstanding when the holidays arrived.

I went on my visitation outing and enjoyed myself. I then boarded the bus for my return to the base, when an uncommon snowfall caused the bus to be delayed in Greenville, North Carolina. The passengers were advised to disembark, find overnight lodging, and to consult with the bus station the next day.

I elected to wander around the area blocks looking for an inexpensive hotel where I could spend the night in this unfamiliar setting. My search, ill-advisedly, led me to a nearby seemingly Black neighborhood. Dressed in uniform, I knew I stood out as I heard the steps of two young Black men who appeared to be following me. The street and sidewalks were empty of other travelers when I heard the quickening steps behind as they attempted to attack me. My quick response and my Judo defense shortly ended the skirmish. The activity was noted by someone who called the police. A copy of the incident report was given to me. The police also assisted me in finding lodging for the night. I returned to the base the next evening.

Upon my reentry, I was detained and advised that my absence had been classified as an AWOL offense. I was to be court marshaled as a result of the reporting by the sergeant who was trying to get me to reenlist. After spending a night in jail, I was released to return to my barracks until summoned for a hearing on my court martial. I was advised that legal assistance was available to me, which I declined. Shortly after, I was notified of my scheduled court appearance.

In uniform, I was ushered into the courtroom where the proceedings would occur under the auspices of the hearing officer. There were a few other people present when the court reporter announced my case. The sergeant was asked to address the court and present the charges against me. I was shocked when the sergeant said I had a long list of issues where I was disrespectful to my superiors, failed to maintain my bunk area properly, and violated my leave provisions, as evidenced by my late return to my duty station. These were just a few of the disciplinary problems the sergeant said I had exhibited during my assignment.

I listened in disbelief as the sergeant concluded the summation of charges. When the sergeant finished, the hearing officer asked me what I had to say for myself.

I rebutted the charges and also provided a copy of the police report about the incident in Greenville to the hearing officer. Upon closer inspection, I recognized the team manager for the ball team in Japan. The case was summarily dismissed. My G.A. had come to my rescue again.

This incident did not leave a bad taste in my mouth. I had embraced the military and recognized the on-going benefits and related experiences that resulted in the view that all eligible young men could benefit from the draft. I remain proud and pleased with my military exposure, inclusive of it serving as a vehicle for traveling to various states and the world. It provided me with the opportunity to experience the culture of a different country.

While in Japan, I used some of my income to purchase a substantial wardrobe (Italian silk suits) and slide rules. I subsequently sold the slide rules in front of the college bookstore after offering a price below the price in the store, and only after I changed the price to be more than the store price. I was able to sell my supply and pocket a substantial return on my untested notion of marketing. This period of time served as an internship prior to my entry into the private sector, and would influence the balance of my life.

Part II
Entering the World of Work

David Long

After the Military

I was able to complete my three-year tenure without further conflicts. I received my honorable discharge and returned to Winston-Salem. I had decided to evaluate the area as an option in the execution of my game plan.

I stayed with my aunt. While living there, I visited several college campuses and examined the curriculums they offered. They were in the middle of their semester year. This gave me ample time to make a decision.

My cousin was a registered nurse who also lived in Winston-Salem, with her doctor husband. The doctor invited me to assist him with paperwork and billing processes related to the operation of his office and general practice.

In the absence of any other obligations or impediments, I joined them in their practice. These temporary experimental and related experiences were shortly terminated when I received a phone call informing me of a family crisis. My mom was prepared to kill my dad for unspecified reasons, and I was needed at home. This summons warranted my immediate attention, as I packed hastily for the trip back home. In this process, I learned that my older brother had reenlisted and was stationed at a military base in Virginia.

East Boogie Again

On the bus trip home, I wondered what miraculous powers it was presumed I had that might enable me to unlock the psychological underpinnings of my parent's distress. I was nobody's psychiatrist. I knew there were some risks involved, but I also knew that the three-year separation had invited my exposure to a few things in life.

A modest bag of experiences ranged from an introduction to the field of aviation, tech training on various electronic devices, and volumes of rules, regulations, and legal applications in adjudicating the non-adherence to same. I knew I had only scratched the surface of any number of disciplines and vocations.

This crisis was interfering and interrupting my own pursuit of excellence and invited the deviation from my master plan. My anxiety invoked the reality that I had left the house as a young boy, but now I was returning as a male adult. I did have my spikes and gloves in my luggage as part of my arsenal of available resources, inclusive of my unknown G.A.

My unannounced arrival was greeted cordially. My brothers were happy to see me. I was quickly assigned to my older brother's unoccupied bedroom. At least my older brother was smart enough to not return.

The Beat Goes On

As I attempted to ease into my old environment, I could not avoid observing some other issues. I saw the decline of the meat packing industry. Several plants had announced their closure and Swift's (Dad's plant) had been scaled back. The city had changed. It appeared older and smaller than what it used to be.

There was the appearance of other unmet needs and little activity in the downtown area and neighborhoods. When I re-visited and attended my church, I was quickly embraced and advised that they needed a Sunday school teacher for the teens. I accepted this invitation and soon became the superintendent. I also began trying to teach my brothers and other neighborhood kids some of the basics of my boot camp experiences, i.e. fundamentals of marching.

I was pleasantly surprised when one of my applications for employment was accepted by a conveniently located utility company (Union Electric) in the nearby downtown area of St. Louis. I was informed that I should attend a Friday afternoon meeting for an orientation and introduction to this job opportunity.

On that Friday, I was directed to the supervisor of the work area where I would be working as an office boy. After introductions, the supervisor proceeded to show me around the area and informed me of their ideas and expectations.

Orientation at Union Electric

My first day of orientation at Union Electric (UE) covered everything from A-Z. When the supervisor noticed my watch, it hurt my feelings when he asked me if I could tell time. He further tested my agility and strength by asking me to lift and place several boxes on different shelves. Break times and work attire were also addressed. He pointed out to me a little old man sitting in the corner of the room that had not been late for work for the past 20 years. He asked if I had any questions. Having none, he left me with a closing reminder of my hours of 8 a.m. until closing at 4:30 p.m.

The bus trip home involved a ride across the bridge and then transferring to another bus. I was quietly pleased with myself and quickly determined that I would restrain myself and withhold any celebratory notions until sometime in the future.

I would prepare myself for my first day, on my first real job, for the following Monday, including making a trial run by bus to ensure timeliness.

Monday morning, I caught the bus as planned. When I transferred to the second bus, it stopped abruptly in the middle of the bridge. Trapped in traffic, my efforts to get off the bus were rebuffed.

When I reached the office some two hours later, my supervisor was standing in front of the entrance, arms folded, and blocking my entry into the workplace. In spite of my travels, training, and prior experiences, nothing had prepared me for a moment like this.

The supervisor raised his arms in dismay while my coworkers looked on. "Long! Long!" he shouted. "What do you have to say for yourself? Did I not tell you what time to be here?"

As he continued to shout, that's when I whispered, "Do you see that man over there in the corner?"

"What about him?" the supervisor asked.

Rather than yell back, I continued to diffuse the situation by keeping my voice low. "You won't have to worry about me breaking his 20-year perfect attendance record." (Aha! My G.A.)

In amazement, the supervisor looked at me and said, "Oh, just go to work!" He was subsequently commended for the manner in which he handled my tardiness.

Post First Day

At the time I was hired, I did not know I was among the first few Black employees Union Electric hired. Barriers of segregation were being softened.

After only about three months of working, I told my dad of my plan to quit my job and go to college full-time. Dad had me to show him one of my check stubs. He placed one of his own check stubs on the kitchen table and asked me to look at both of them.

A quick review revealed I was making more money as an office boy than my dad made as a laborer during his 20 plus years at the meat packing plant. How could they do that to him?

A lightbulb came on in my head. I understood things a lot better now. My mother's complaints, my dad's meager wardrobe, etcetera. I told my dad that I was going to the plant that night and set it on fire.

Dad placed his hand on my shoulder and pleaded with me to calm down. He went on to explain to me how much he, and other Black employees, needed these types of jobs, particularly in light of their limitations. Consequently, I was advised not to carry out the threat to burn the plant down.

"What I would rather you do is to keep that white man's job and go to school at night. You're not married. There's nothing preventing you from doing both," my dad told me.

I told him I would think about his suggestion. I wasn't sure I had calmed down after the revelation just made known to me.

Re-Awakening

Fall semester registration was a few weeks away. I learned that the main campus of Southern Illinois University was located in Carbondale, Illinois. They were in the process of establishing an urban focused college in Edwardsville, Illinois. In this regard, they would be temporarily occupying my old high school pending the construction of the new campus. I decided to enroll at this developing new college and keep my job for the immediate future.

My dad, however, fell back into his pattern of assigning chores for all in spite of my financial support. He ignored my challenges of holding a job and the burden of college classes and related homework in the evenings. Something had to give, so I moved out of the Long household and rented a small house with one of my classmates.

Over the span of the ensuing three years, I established the foundational bricks for my future.

- Purchased my first car
- Joined an investment club
- Acquired the mortgages for two rental units
- Continued my commitment to my church
- Joined a choral club – representing the city

While enjoying my first year on the job, I was often stopped by the receptionist. She had not been informed that a few Blacks had been added to the overall staffing.

This information may not have helped deal with a confrontation I had with a security officer picking up receipts from the cafeteria. Upon seeing me inside the building, quickly stopped, drew his pistol and pointed his gun at me.

Rather than turning to flee, I continued toward the officer. In a loud voice for others to hear, I said, "Man, you have a great quick draw! Would you show me that again?" My G.A. was doing his thing.

There were other matters that occurred, such as learning that the company car I routinely drove was being reported as a possible stolen company car.

I was further disappointed when I did not receive a key for the restrooms. This was because the doors to the executive restrooms were being removed, to which the other executives credited me for the loss of this amenity.

There was no plan to educate the workforce of the company's integration steps and measures. To its credit, the company adjusted other policies that promoted the removal of barriers to their integration initiatives. Their efforts included the removal of barriers to the Country Club located in Fenton, Missouri and eliminating access barriers to its health programs

Return to the Master Plan

I told myself that I was making progress on my master plan. At college, I learned, although the architectural school had not been established, over a 10-year period, in the interim, I had accumulated more than enough credits to receive an MBA degree.

During this period, I had mixed reviews of several of the professors who appeared to be troubled by my presence. One professor, offended by my front row election, suggested I sit in the back of the class. I did not abide by his directive. Another instructor acknowledged that he was aware of his reputation as being one of the harshest instructors on campus. He was known to give only one 'A' and maybe a 'B' or two. At the end of his pronouncements, the professor asked if there were any questions. I raised my hand, and indicated that while I did not have a question I had a comment. I told him I would be his one 'A' student.

On another occasion, there was an encounter I had with a staff professor from Africa. He had me stay after the close of the first night of class, at which time he told me that in his view, Black people in America had been corrupted by the white man's blood. Being a pure African, he stated I should know that he was superior to me and that I should not hold out any notion that we might have something in common.

I diffused this situation by informing the professor that I had the upmost respect for all of my professors and would earn every bit of the "A" grade I was accustomed to receiving by virtue of my performance in class. My goal was to make my professor proud he had me in his class. I was, however, a little disappointed that the architectural school remained undeveloped, but I did give the university an 'E' for effort.

Early on, I had the experience as an undergrad to complain to my advisor about the biased grading by an English professor. My complaint was supported by two other classmates that I had solicited in my quest for equity. I was encouraged to deal forthright with issues of this nature as opposed to waiting for the close of the semester.

On the home front, I was invited to join a fledgling business operation registered as Muggeridge Manufacturing Company. Under the leadership of my uncle the policeman, this activity involved the production of a variety of cleaning products which would be initially sold locally in area stores. The products were developed by a high school chemistry teacher who took the time to secure patents on the products.

This favored uncle, who I had spent summers with babysitting his kids, took his entrepreneurial skills and spirit to the level of purchasing a neighborhood grocery store. When the store was not realizing the anticipated profits for unknown reasons I was asked to discreetly examine the operation to identify the problems. I advised my uncle that the problem appeared to be related to the security associated with the store, which was under the supervision of a white policeman who was also my uncle's ten-year partner on the police force. Immediately, I was informed that my services would no longer be needed.

A short time later, I learned of an incident involving a white lady who lived across the street from the store. Her son's bike was stolen. My uncle posted a notice of a monetary reward leading to the return of the bike. The reward notice was successful and the bike was returned. In gratitude, the lady discreetly informed my uncle that while it was not her business to meddle in other folks business, she wanted to inform him she noticed, almost on a daily basis, the security guard (my uncle's partner on the police force) placing numerous bags of groceries into the trunk of his car prior to leaving after the close of business. Subsequently, my uncle sought my advice in terms of solving this dilemma. I did so in a manner that did not adversely affect their partnership, and no, the uncle did not offer me an apology. I might mention, he was the first canine officer and I noted his training techniques and approaches on a firsthand basis.

On the job, I was invited to participate in an internal management intern program which involved being exposed to all the major divisions of the company. I encountered several barriers as I progressed through the program. I was also exposed to several of the major home builders in the area, along with a minority neighborhood-based organization led by Mackler Shepard, (Jeff-Vander-Lou, Corporation) in concert with McCormack Baron, a major builder.

I was surprised when I saw myself featured in an exhibit the company had developed for the World Fair in New York (1974-75). I also did not know an exhibit from another county would be shipped back to St.

Louis and located at Broadway and Market Street, referenced as the Spanish Pavilion. I enjoyed the company sponsored trip to the fair.

The company further had an Executive Loan Program wherein they would permit the staff to assist the communities they were serving. I participated in this initiative as a loaned executive to my hometown of East St. Louis. Then came the innocent mishap that changed my life and vision…and it came to pass.

I did not know the new and first Black mayor of my hometown had requested assistance via the Executive Loan Program and had specifically requested my assistance. Consequently, after pausing to consider the unknowns, I agreed to embark upon this new endeavor. This entailed a sober assessment regarding the challenges of such an undertaking. I had to be different and let it be known that I intended to be a positive change agent, inclusive of introducing a different culture for the new environment. The timing appeared to be right in light of a new city mayor. In addition, I would be sacrificing the now thirteen years of employment since I was two years short of the fifteen-year requirement threshold.

My thoughts included some other prior and related incidents. Trying to return home from work one evening, my normal patterns were interrupted by barricades in my neighborhood, making access to my carport uncommonly awkward and tedious. A community organizer, I learned, was having a meeting with area homeowners announcing he would be representing the area where I resided regarding a new federal program. Of course, I was unimpressed with the appearance, language, and overall demeanor of the organizer.

In addition, I had an earlier encounter with the precinct committee-man who had removed a parking ticket off of my car. The committee-man claimed he could easily take care of the ticket, but it would entail me accompanying him downtown to handle the matter.

I did not know this person would stroll into court while court was in session with me in tow and the ticket in hand. He announced that he needed the judge to do something. The judge in return, directed the bailiff to remove both of us from his courtroom.

More than embarrassed, I knew that I would not be satisfied with the limited person representing me. I determined to do something about it.

Shortly after that incident, I was selected to represent my neighborhood. Later I was selected to be the chairman for all of the neighborhoods. In this capacity, the city director would submit reports to me. Monthly meetings were held with me and other board members regarding this program referred to as the Model Cities Program.

Public meetings were typically held in the evenings, in a city owned facility, adjacent to city hall. At a *standing room only* meeting, a local militant approached the conference table, sat down across from the director, removed a pistol from his waistband, and announced that he was going to shoot the director.

Suddenly, the meeting room went empty, leaving the director, the militant, and me at the conference table. I would have retreated too had I not noticed that the militant was so upset that the gun he was holding wavered between me and the director.

The director was silent as the militant registered his complaint against the director. For fear of any quick movement on my part that might invite unwanted attention, I remained in my seat. I told the militant that no business could be discussed until he put his gun away. My voice was stern, yet calming and forceful.

The militant indicated he did not want to put the gun away. I proceeded to explain that this was a prerequisite prior to any discussion.

Reluctantly, the militant put his gun away and I resumed the meeting with the caveat that the director address and resolve the concerns of the militant. Those present agreed not to disclose this incident to the media, the Mayor, or the public. My G.A. remained consistent.

Sometime later, the director decided to relinquish his position. He may have recommended me as the ideal candidate to succeed him. However, there was never a discussion concerning the director's plans, much less any recommendations involving me.

Consequently, I was surprised when my supervisor informed me that my talents had been requested by the mayor of East Boogie. I did not know this change of venue would entail the formulation of values with Biblical underpinnings, i.e. treating clients and fellow taxpayers with respect, making them the more important part of the equation, and providing loving care in the delivery of services and assistance. These notions would be negatively compounded in relationship to Blacks ascending to greater political power and the belief that they were in greater charge of how things might be done, with indeed the opportunity to line their own pockets, employ their family and friends, and engage in all manner of misdeeds like they felt their predecessors had done. It, perhaps, was equivalent to the ravished dogs that broke the lock on the meat house door, and having their master advise them that they should not eat the meat as the saga unfolded regarding issues of malfeasance, thefts, and other expressions of greed.

David Long

Model City Program

After three days of silent meditation and soul-searching, I advised my employer that I would accept the challenge to assist my hometown via the Executive Loan Program. This was in spite of the known factors and notwithstanding the evolving job duties. I also elected to consult with my college advisor. I had to put on my shield of protection and rely upon my G.A. This determination, in retrospect, resulted in the most dynamic period (7 years) of my career. Little did I know of the ensuing background checks and scrutiny of my activities that included the tapping of my home and office phones. A bank official cohort advised that the bank was required to avail a key to my safety deposit box for the review of its contents.

Many other factors entered my mindset regarding the notion of becoming the second Model City director, which would entail moving the impetus of the program from a series of pacification initiatives to a series of initiatives that might promote a *do it yourself* approach in alleviating the effects of economic decline and urban stress. My new office was to be located in the vault area of a donated bank building. I quietly began to implement the following initiatives:

- Clean-up
- City operated demolition program to remove dilapidated buildings
- Energy efficient measures to reduce energy costs for individual homes

- Installation of sewers in unserved neighborhoods
- New fire stations
- Neighborhood health clinics
- Head Start program for kids
- Police Community Relations Program
- Skill development in basic vocations (i.e., typing)
- Economic development to assist small businesses
- Katherine Dunham Dance Program

It is doubtful that the citizens of East St. Louis would know that my legacy includes:

- The present City Hall
- Two fire-stations in the south end
- Sewers for the south end of the city
- Mary Brown Community Center
- Location of the State Community College
- Why the Illinois State Office Building faces eastward
- Why Popular Street Bridge exits onto Tudor Avenue and stops abruptly at 13th Street
- Highly visible Parsons Place Apartments parallel I-64 in Emerson Park neighborhood

I championed the conversion to the aldermanic form of government as contrasted with the weak mayor council form of government. I also addressed the absence of a reference to the east side of the Mississippi River regarding the St. Louis Arch's development, which is now filled by a promenade and geyser fountain in East St. Louis (adjacent to the Casino Queen presently referenced as Malcomb W. Memorial Park). The fountains can lift water up to 630' equal to the height of the Arch.

NBC-LEO representatives asked me to participate in a unique orientation for new mayors, i.e. Maynard Jackson who subsequently tried to woo me to Atlanta on three different occasions.

I would be remiss in not acknowledging that my experience in East Boogie was a labor of love for my community. Yet, I knew I was confronted with insurmountable odds from the community when I attempted to cope with exigencies of changes in, and to, the city's dwindling tax base. This was due to the exodus of white flight, particularly the resulting pressure on the public sector and the temptation of nepotism.

I could also be reminded of other minor incidents. For instance, my secretary informed me that the mayor and a small group of others wanted to meet with me. To accommodate this unscheduled meeting, extra chairs were brought into the vaulted chambers. I offered the director's chair and desk for the mayor's use.

I took a seat, the door was secured, and the mayor announced he would be conducting an informal inquiry regarding a complaint registered against me. The attending aldermen would serve as the jurors/jury in this hearing. The complaint stated I had made several inappropriate remarks to one of my female employees who was married. Her husband was present and was representing his wife in this regard.

The mayor asked what I had to say for myself. I quietly advised that at no one time did I engage in any activity that might compromise my office or embarrass the mayor. I indicated that I was unaware of an expressed concern regarding this employee, yet I went on to acknowledge that there had been a minor personnel matter that had arisen within my office. This matter was related to one of my male secretaries being crowned as the "queen" of the annual Miss Fannie's Ball. This male employee had pictures of the crown and proudly informed his co-workers of the contest and his success. I noticed the disruption to the normal activity of the office, but the staff assured me that the excitement would be curtailed and they would get back to work.

Shortly thereafter, I was informed by several other female employees that a problem had arisen. The male winner of the Miss Fannie's Ball had elected to use the women's restroom, and they wanted me to intervene. I responded that everyone had to work together and that I would leave it up to all the females in the office to resolve the matter. The wife of the husband, who was now complaining, disapproved of my decision.

I also noted that the female employee did not take advantage of the office's grievance procedure nor the city's personnel department regarding this matter. Finally, although the complainant was in violation of the city's residency requirement, I trusted this would be shortly clarified.

With these concluding remarks, the mayor asked if there were any questions. Hearing none, he asked the woman's husband and me to leave the hearing. The determination of the hearing would be shortly announced. Fifteen minutes later, I was advised that I could return to my office and that the matter had been dismissed.

The following day, I was invited to visit the mayor's office. The mayor appeared to be in good spirits as he welcomed me to his office and closed the door. He told me I had passed the "test." Also, it had been determined that I should develop an innovative project that would establish a secretarial pool for the support of various offices within city hall. Indeed, I would be expected to attest to the T&A's and related payroll costs, even though I might not see the employees of the pool. Finally, I would be expected to discreetly support this endeavor that would involve a supervisor who would provide directions for the pool. The mayor advised me that I was now being invited to attend bi-weekly meetings of the political organization.

Reflections

I was reminded of my days in Japan, when the U.S. military was in charge and determined how they would conduct themselves. I agreed to develop the project of special interest to the Mayor and informed him that I would attend a few of the organization's meetings.

I was subsequently visited by the head of the organization and asked to be on a joint ballot for two positions on a pending school board election. The organization would bear all the advertising costs and my picture would be in the campaign literature. I also conducted my own campaign.

At campaign headquarters, I was welcomed and given access to the tabulation of the election votes. I was informed that I had won the election for a seat on the Board of Education, however, it would be reported to the media and general public that I had lost.

Sometime later, one of my brothers ran for public office. His brother's opponent died before the election. A meeting was held with my brother and representatives of the organization. My brother declined assistance from the organization and advised the representatives that he did not need them, since he was the only remaining candidate on the ballot.

At the end of the election, my brother learned that he had not won the election. A write-in candidate, supported by the organization, received more votes.

One of my cousins also decided to run for a public office. At the end of the election it was reported that my cousin did not receive any votes. I called the organization headquarters and was told my cousin had not won the election, although at least two ballots that appeared to be votes for my cousin were determined to be spoiled by the election judges and subsequently discarded.

Upon deeper reflections, the reality of my experiences as the local administrator of federal funds (trying to ensure the integrity of dollars spent) reveals that I did keep the faith in spite of program expenditures beyond my control.

I would be remiss in not acknowledging that my manhood was tested in terms of wine, women, and partying. My naiveté was brought home to me when a local paint contractor and neighbor came to my office with a case of liquor. This, I learned, was my cut from the job I had awarded to him for painting our office interior. I was confused because I negotiated the contract properly and there was no hint of any impropriety or kickbacks, yet the contractor was advised that in order to get paid, he was to reward certain offices/persons. I found out these instructions were coming from our own fiscal department. This explained other disturbances within the office that had occurred involving this one financial/fiscal staffer.

Also, there was the incident early on in the mayor's office. An alderman publicly complained that he felt that his ward was not being treated on an equitable basis. He had a truck to dump a deposit in front of City Hall as an expression of his displeasure. On the evening prior to the council meeting, all of the aldermen and a few departmental heads were present to go over the agenda. These meetings were closed to the press.

All the aldermen came dressed (armed with pistols) for the meeting and indeed the alderman voiced his complaint again. It was indicated that his complaint should be directed to me as the director of the program. We were sitting in a circle in front of the mayor's desk when the alderman appeared in front of me with his verbal tirade. It appeared as if he was about to lose control as he raised his voice and started swaying back and forth.

My military training was activated and before I knew it, the 'blow' caught him in his solar plexus. The alderman fell backwards, across the mayor's desk, and into the mayor's lap. Several other aldermen grabbed and restrained me. As a professional, they reminded me that I was not to respond in the manner that I did. The meeting was subsequently recalled to order and we were kept apart for the balance of the meeting.

When I made my department report the following night, the mayor requested a motion on the disposition of my report. All eyes focused in on the complaining alderman as he announced that whatever I wanted in regard to the report, he was in favor of. We became buddies thereafter.

When Little R got busted for the demonstration demotion program (the checks were made out to fictitious companies and were all endorsed by Little R, each in the amount of $10,000), I was taken aside and advised that it was my job to not allow others to embarrass themselves in that manner. Furthermore, the other alderman wanted my sit-down as a result. I quietly disagreed and tried to make it known that my job description did not indicate, nor did I have the authority to protect others from themselves.

I was not available for their indiscreet parties and reminded all that I was satisfied marching to the beat of different music and other songs. The presence of the federal program also generated negative impacts inclusive of several deaths, shoot-outs, along with one unexplained death as a result of a fall off the Popular Street Bridge. In retrospect, the authorities seemingly ignored the fleecing of the city while under white control, resulting in the white exodus of businesses, jobs, and people to the surrounding communities. This seemingly encouraged the development of the 'black hole.'

There was also the appearance of an invisible wall that coincided with the limits of the city that seemed to be destined for self-destruction. The community was ill-equipped with no defense against nepotism and graft, and scarce resources for training of staff. This was in addition to the absence of formal development of political leadership.

I wonder if some of my suggestions, i.e. establishing distressed cities as military resource providers (consumable supplies, uniforms, etc.) might be a viable strategy. In spite of these observations and reservations, I was passionate and loyal to my superiors. I experienced a stake holding reality heretofore unavailable. In my capacity as director, I initiated a year end celebration featuring the successes and achievements of the Model City Program. I credited others, including the mayor's office, with being responsible for the attainments being recognized. The funding office soon noticed this effort and promoted similar observances on a nationwide basis.

Mt. Pisgah

My relationship with Mt. Pisgah Church covered a period in excess of thirty years. It included being a member of the young adult choir, a Sunday school teacher, the superintendent of Sunday school, and serving on the board of trustees as its secretary.

I was intimately involved in the relocation of the church from 2nd Street to 13th and Summit. I was instrumental in overcoming the collapse of the ceiling roof and retiring the mortgage for the facility.

It can be noted that the pastor, Dr. Robert Lyles, served as president of the Illinois State Baptist Convention and was cited in a casebook study presented at Harvard University and written by A. M. Warrock (under the direction of A. Altshuler, Professor of Urban Policy & Planning & M. Zegans, executive director of the Program on Innovations in state and local governments, for use at the J.F. Kennedy School of Government). The study revealed Dr. Lyles role in the "One Church One Child" program where a church would adopt one child. This has since been encouraged on a nationwide basis. This came to my attention through my participation in a 1997 seminar at Harvard University.

The initial reception entailed the discovery of feces sprinkled in the linen cabinets. Also, I didn't want to say a thing about the visiting professor's dissertation explaining the term "blastomania." This term connoted the ungratefulness of slaves, in spite of their benefits, as well as the non-recognition of their owner's investment in slaves and their audacity to succumb to the overwhelming desire to flee. Since the slave owners could not comprehend this phenomenon, it was referred to as blastomania.

Earlier, I noticed the absence of minority professors on the staff of my university of choice (Southern Illinois University at Edwardsville, Illinois), along with the absence of courses addressing the ethical influence upon the practitioners in our society. How could my white classmate, who admitted his racist orientation, accept employment as a service provider for minority clients? I knew that I might not want to dwell on my white classmates' burdens since I did not want to ask how a person can maintain polar opposites and yet be comfortable within themselves. I was encouraged through a consulting visitation to East Boogie by several Black professors from the University of Pittsburgh, and my dad's ethos, wherein you pick your own Waterloo.

John H. Johnson Boys' Club

Over a seven-year period, I engaged in my own social experiment and special project. This experiment was related to the notion that young Black boys had become an endangered species. Many of us are familiar with the following story about Little Johnny.

Little Johnny was asked by the principal at his third grade graduation, how many days are there in a week. Little Johnny, counting on his fingers said, "Seven."

"That's good, Johnny. Now tell me how many days of the week start with the letter T."

Johnny said, "Two."

The principal said, "That's great, Johnny. Now, what are they?"

Johnny paused for a moment and said, "Today and tomorrow."

The principal said, "The program is about to begin. Let's find some seats."

This experiment was the consequence of a chance encounter with a Black man who was visiting with several vehicles looking for parking spaces on the St. Louis riverfront with his son in tow. I made the mistake of asking the man what he was doing. The man said he was teaching his son how to beg at an early age.

His response disturbed me. Why would any parent elect to set that type of example for their child? There had to be other options. If so, what might they look like or what might be done to introduce basic skills to one's offspring? This resulted in my idea for a club for young boys between the ages of 8 and 16, from a mixture of incomes, single parent or two parent homes, and not to exceed 24 in the number of participants. Classes could be conducted in my home on Saturdays and would not exceed two hours in length.

The agenda for the meeting would be focused on the letter H – Heart, Head, and Hand. The first H was defined as being related to one's dreams. The second H was defined as one's mental capacity, and the third H was defined as activities associated with the use of one's hands.

The trick to these three H objectives required that the related goals had to be different in order to enhance the overall abilities of the individual. No donations would be accepted, and a business plan would be developed to generate income for the club.

The business plan incorporated some of the basic principles of management, i.e. planning, organizing, directing, controlling and evaluation of one's activities. The underlying premise entailed the search for one's purpose in life with related Christian-based values and the published "Maslow's Theory." Speakers, such as a mail carrier, fireman, policeman, sanitation engineer, plumber, public health official, barber, male nurse, and electrical journeyman, were placed on the agenda.

Emphasis was placed on self-love and the notion that scarcity invited value, as in diamonds. Role modeling and sales presentations were practiced along with the influence of several Black professors from Pittsburgh. Local outings included trips to a funeral home, jail, and vocational schools.

At the end of the summer, sales income from activities, i.e. selling candy, cleaning products, light bulbs, washing cars, and taking meat orders enabled me to charter a bus for weeklong outings to places like Georgia, Florida, Wisconsin Dells, Indiana, Nashville, Chicago, and the Houston Space Station. While there was an attrition rate of 50%, I was pleased with my successful experiment and the lessons learned by the kids as I benefitted from these efforts also.

One of the more important lessons taught during this period of time involved the view that policemen could be a friend as opposed to an enemy. Police officers should be given the respect that the uniform invited. In communicating, sir or ma'am would be appropriate. If told to stop...do so and face the officer with raised hands, palms forward, so that it would be clear that you do not have a lethal instrument (put down anything you may have been holding). Ask how YOU can assist the officer.

These steps should be carried out slowly. If you need to show identification, and need to retrieve it, inform the officer that you need to retrieve your ID. Step by step, let the officer know what you are doing to retrieve it. This approach tends to diffuse what could be an otherwise volatile situation. This is the opposite of the impulse or the effort to run. Few people are fast enough to outrun a speeding bullet. Note, not only should Black lives matter but all lives should matter. Police officers mask their fears too.

Discipline was an implied assumption and prerequisite. Alternatively, and in my view, sparing the rod invites spoiling of the child, along with other undesirable traits and characteristics. This can result in handicapping the child and creating other barriers to their full development.

It is not uncommon for new parents to subconsciously follow the patterns of their parents while trying to be a parent and friend. It's a tight rope to walk. It typically does not work out in relationship to correcting their mistakes.

A spoiled child believes the world owes him/her everything because he/she is so special. All they need to do is let the parent know what it is that they want. A more appropriate approach would involve comparing unconditional love versus conditional love where balance or equilibrium becomes the desired outcome. This view is taken in relationship to perceiving the child as the victim and the zealous loving parent handicapping the victim to the extent that the victim is seldom, if ever, able to overcome unanticipated barriers in their development.

Notwithstanding the three-prong approach (the three H's), if there remains an overwhelming compulsion to do something, you can always teach the child other positive things. It can be noted that this experiment was in response to one father's search to equip others with some basic tools that turned out to be successful.

These positive and productive experiences did not result in the notion that I was now an expert, but simply underscored the unmet needs in this area of education. It might aid a single parent in facilitating his/her offspring to become the best they can be. In addition, it might help to compensate for the missing mate and address unknown purposes in the lives of the single parent's offspring.

I incorporated the notion that we are products of our environment and represent the accumulated experiences we might have had. I focused upon providing different positive outlets and travel as a means of enhancing the knowledge of my students in their quest to determine what skills and talents they possessed.

I also noticed that we always had trouble getting one of the boys to volunteer to be locked up in a coffin (last resting place). We, therefore, had not one boy, but all of the boys, go through the planned abbreviated booking process at the police station, including a brief incarceration period after being photographed in a mock line-up.

The following expressions served as underpinnings for the club:

I Have Only Just A Minute
Dr. Benjamin East Mays

I have only just a minute,
Only sixty seconds in it.
Forced upon me, can't refuse it.
But it's up to me to use it.
I must suffer if I lose it.
Give account if I abuse it.
Just a tiny little minute,
but eternity is in it.

Myself
Edgar Guest

I have to live with myself and so

I want to be fit for myself to know.

I want to be able as days go by,

always to look myself straight in the eye.

I don't want to stand with the setting sun

and hate myself for the things I have done.

I don't want to keep on a closet shelf

a lot of secrets about myself

and fool myself as I come and go

into thinking no one else will ever know

the kind of person I really am.

I don't want to dress up myself in sham.

I want to go out with my head erect

I want to deserve all men's respect;

but here in the struggle for fame and wealth

I want to be able to like myself.

I don't want to look at myself and know

I am bluster and bluff and empty show.

I never can hide myself from me;

David Long

I see what others may never see;
I know what others may never know,
I never can fool myself and so,
whatever happens I want to be
self-respecting and conscience free.

Part III
The Civil Servant Years

HUD @ ST. LOUIS

In 1979, a new city mayor was elected for East Boogie. I determined that it was, in spite of the successes of the program, time to submit my resignation. I was reminded that early on (when I first joined the city's rank and file) there were many times at the end of the day, I would retreat with the realization that my progress was related to what I had prevented from happening as compared to some milestone of achievement. I smiled to myself regarding the mayor's appointee who, after listening to the report concerning the slow pace of the demolition program due to the difficulties of tracking down the owners and heirs of now vacant properties, announced he could solve such issues quite easily as he reached into his pocket, pulled out a match, and struck it.

There were some good days, and a spirit of quiet exhilaration reflective of a stakeholding interest in the various outcomes addressing the myriad issues of the day. My influence was far reaching. My programmatic efforts touched on all aspects of governing a city.

Around the seventh year, I was sitting next to the mayor in the VIP section of some temporary bleachers brought in to celebrate the ground breaking of the new city hall. The mayor complained that he preferred and wanted the approval of his first preference, which was an application for funding a sewer system for a small portion of the city crafted under the direction of my white administrative assistant (compared to my application which was selected and funded).

94

I knew, once again, it was time for others to take on the unending challenges so I submitted my resignation to the new mayor. The construction and completion of the new city hall would become my final gift to my beloved city. It could also be noted that the administration of the program was subsequently transferred to Belleville, Illinois due to on-going issues in the management of the program not too long after my departure.

Shortly thereafter, my dad passed away. I unknowingly fell into a deep depression and was aroused, several months later, by a recruiter from the Kansas City HUD office who encouraged me to accept an opportunity to work at the federal level with the Department of Housing and Urban Development (DHUD). This would alter my previous years of searching for resources and federal dollars to a position of giving away the resources that I had been routinely seeking.

My orientation was under the leadership of the first Black female head secretary of DHUD. She had a distinguished legal background and roots in Chicago, my hometown sister-city. Central to the challenges she wanted to address the preposterous notion of changing the culture of the agency's 10,000 plus employees. This would entail a new administrative emphasis, a performance-based delivery system of the agency's programs, and the provision of technical assistance to grant recipients with a concurrent emphasis upon goal attainments.

It was acknowledged that many field offices were enjoying a somewhat lackadaisical approach to their responsibilities and were quite comfortable in awaiting their personal retirements. As change-agents, we were to somehow overcome the existing malaise and invite attention to the preferred productivity emphasis. Little did I know of the curious reception awaiting me and the other new staffer assigned to the St. Louis office.

With little fanfare, upon my arrival at St. Louis, I was greeted with a small luncheon attended by several members of top management. After the standard introduction, the burning question was asked in a number of ways, i.e., who I dealt with, who did I know, and what would I be doing, particularly since management officials in the St. Louis office were not included in the selection process, something which had been the past practice.

Back at the office, I was further accorded visitations with the other divisional directors in their normal work environments. One immaculately attired director welcomed me to his office. He proceeded to quickly advise, if I wanted to know what his division did that I would have to schedule a meeting with the Black female he designated to be responsible for the work of the office since he did not have a clue. While talking, he adjusted his cufflinks and then asked me to join him in a cup of coffee.

My assignment was as the program manager as opposed to the assistant director or deputy director of one particular division. Indeed, it was quietly pointed out that the director was a registered member of Mensa– a select group of persons with the highest IQs. I was informed that my new boss had never made a bad decision in his life, predicated upon him receiving the appropriate background information.

As I examined and analyzed the modus-operandi of the office, I was greeted with remarks from my new staff. "I guess you have to be a chocolate drop to get ahead around here," I heard someone say as they routinely visited the divisional coffee pot area. Where had I heard similar remarks before?

For several weeks, it appeared that I was doing very little. My director would stick his head into my cubicle. Upon noticing that I was creating an organizational chart with internal reporting responsibilities, the director mentioned he would like to know what the two program assistants could be doing, since they routinely requested overtime.

I began conducting individual consultations with my new staff, armed with my organizational chart. One PhD staffer advised me that she had contacts with the regional office and could easily have my testicles removed should I believe that I could tell her what to do. The male engineer indicated that I would receive his full support. The reality was that I had to familiarize myself with the job responsibilities of each of my subordinates, and ensure I had sufficient skills to perform their jobs in their absence. I would also be expected to evaluate their performance. These included CPD reps, specialist positions, along with an engineer, environmental and financial officers, and secretaries. This determination did not include the myriad programs assigned to this division of HUD nor knowledge of the participating clients.

I began to dismantle the effects of Jim Crow policies via the office's policy of individual travel consideration, as opposed to team travel provisions. I introduced, among the other monitoring policies, a provision that discouraged family outings as an ancillary consideration accorded the traveler. This was related to my assessment of earlier travel experiences with other members of the office.

The team approach resulted in me and my boss travelling together and occupying the same hotel room. It was then that I discovered my boss's liquor dependence. At one point, my boss kept butting his head on the TV stand above the dresser where the bar had been set-up. I intervened and recommended that the bar area be moved to another location. I determined to adjust my new travel policy to accommodate individual hotel accommodations. I also was offered access to the car trunk of my financial analyst's car for drink replenishments as her husband was travelling with her. I subsequently learned that the husband was generating the financial reports she had been forwarding.

Two separate events occurred within the next several months. I elected to intervene upon learning that a fellow HUD staffer was being held hostage by a disgruntled social security recipient who in fact, had gotten off on the wrong floor of the federal building and had mistakenly taken the HUD staffer as hostage. In diffusing this awkward matter, I encouraged the hostage taker to use the emergency exit at the back of the building in order to avoid a confrontation with the police who had been called.

The other incident involved an unscheduled visit by a local militant group who conducted a sit-in with their canine pets and the local news media representatives to record the anticipated confrontation.

The security office informed the office manager of this approaching problem, which he could not restrain. The office manager fled his office and retreated to the chief legal advisor's office. I got a brief phone call telling me I was to handle the pending problem descending upon the manager's office. Without thinking, I put on my suit coat, went out, met with the protesters and diffused the situation without incident. My G.A. (God/guardian angel) had followed me to my new job.

I received a follow-up call from the manager. I was to attest, via a notarized report, that what I did was under his direction and ongoing instructions which led to the militant's peaceful retreat. The regional office had assumed that as they watched the breaking news that the manager would be the one representing the office rather than me. Nonetheless, I signed the report prepared for my signature seemingly detailing the role of the manager in resolving this concern.

There were several other things that happened. I was invited to meet with my divisional director after the closure of normal hours of operations. I was advised to come dressed to protect myself.

I kept the appointment and assured the director that he had nothing to fear from me, as my job was to make him look good. Sometime later, I made good on my commitment when the director attended an out-of-state disaster meeting and somehow lost all of his notes. I was asked to prepare his report for him, which I did. The office manager commended the director for the excellence of the report. The divisional director told me I would be retained and the other HUD staffer that arrived with me would be discharged. This confirmed that I had passed their tests, and was accepted as a viable member of management.

Further, the office manager elected to invite me to participate in the monthly golf outings. No one told me that I was to allow the manager to beat me at golf, and so I failed throughout the golf season to observe the 11th Commandment which might be "Thou shall not beat thy boss at golf" He gave me the impression that I was his show horse.

Then there was the graffiti depicted in the office that resulted in a determination that a Black disgruntled employee was attempting to make the manager look bad as per an external review by the Kansas City office.

As the years began to roll on, the divisional director announced retirement plans. I was charged with formulating the ceremony for the event. After all, I led the office's annual United Way Campaign that resulted in the largest commitment. Since it was my divisional director who was retiring, it was a no brainer.

I learned that my divisional director was disliked by his peers. They had me know that they would do absolutely nothing about his departure and looked forward to his retirement. I reluctantly conveyed the response to the office manager. Despite this resistance, I arranged for the event to be hosted and catered by a nearby downtown hotel.

On the morning of the retirement event, the departing honoree called and advised me that he would be unable to attend. I immediately reported the call to the office manager and asked the manager what I should do. He told me that I had his approval to do whatever I deemed appropriate, as the manager had another appointment to keep himself and would not be present. I elected to continue with the scheduled event and to honor the honoree in his absence. The attendees advised me that the event was one of the best retirement events they had ever attended.

A vacancy notice regarding the now departed director was soon posted. With no movement occurring for the balance of the fiscal year, I naively announced, in the yearly report, that only I could claim the responsibility for the uncommon achievements of the division since I was now the only divisional official. However, I was accorded a telephone interview prior to the arrival of a delegation from the regional office, including the new divisional director. Based on his presence for the final two weeks of the fiscal year, it was reported that this divisional director had immediately enhanced the office, and was credited for the accomplishments I had earlier reported for the current year. The moles had flexed their muscles. I would have to wait for a future opportunity.

Two projects occurred during my watch which brought back memories from my developmental years. One involved the revitalization of an aging excursion boat locally known as the Admiral. Had I heard of this Admiral before? I did not want to ask myself, yet I recommended the approval of funding for this effort.

The other project was referenced as the rebirth of a deteriorated railroad depot known as Union Station. What significance did this project represent in my bank of memories during its heyday? Despite local political and financial oppositions to the project, I reached into my toolbox and successfully assisted in bringing the project online. I received a national architectural award at the end.

Things were moving smoothly as I was elevated to the divisional director's position sometime later. During this period of time, the agency announced a new program for small cities with populations of 50,000 or less. Each field office was assigned the responsibility to provide technical assistance to interested applicants. I took the lead in this regard and conducted several trainings sessions which addressed the criteria and grantsmanship dimensions. For the first two years of the program, applicants from the St. Louis office were cited as the best applications received. Several things occurred upon this realization. One change resulted where the field offices could no longer conduct their own training sessions. Technical representatives identified by headquarters would carry out this responsibility on a nationwide basis. The second change involved the program being assigned to the states themselves, in light of assistance being made available by agency reps of color to this new constituency, which was not appreciated.

In light of these registered complaints, the entire program and process was subsequently awarded to the states for their administration.

My vision extended beyond my responsibilities to my employer. It resulted in me submitting a proposal in response to a competition to identify the best 50 ways to improve St. Louis. It was titled *Let's Make It Better*. This special contest was conducted in 2004 under the auspices of the local newspaper, the St. Louis Post Dispatch and local radio station, KMOX. My proposal was selected as one of the best ideas reviewed.

Breaking news revealed that there had been an unexplained bombing of a federal building in Oklahoma City. Little did I know, but my skillset would be needed in addressing the first known terrorist bombing on U.S. soil.

HUD @ OKC

There was no handbook that the department could refer to or rely on regarding this uncommon problem because of the bombing of the Oklahoma City office. The leadership in D.C. requested volunteers and internally attempted to recruit specific staff to undertake the unknowns of reestablishing the federal presence (HUD office) in OKC. I was promised replacement staff, a new office building, and the latest equipment, all as part of undertaking this new challenge.

By the end of 1995, I made plane reservations and flew into OKC for the first time. In the seat next to me sat a matronly woman who mentioned that she was a native Oklahoman. I shared that this was my first visit to OKC and asked if she would share with me her views of what she liked about OKC. Her quick response was that she liked the pace. According to her, people in OKC were family oriented, supported their kids through their beloved state colleges, were laid back, and quite comfortable maintaining the status quo.

I then asked her to tell me some of the things she disliked. Her response was she disliked the pace. If a person wanted to progress or desired to change things, she said one could easily become frustrated should they be interested in growth and new developments.

This curious assessment would appear to be true as I attempted to get settled in my new environment. I initially accepted an offer from a fellow HUD staffer who I had known for several years, and had previously invited to come for a weekend stay in my hometown. My seamless notions of easing into OKC included a suggestion that we use one car in going back and forth to work. The response was that each should be responsible for their own transportation.

Other observations included noting the civil, cordial, and courteous nature of the people as if the aftermath of the bombing had left or revealed a curious bonding of togetherness and unity. This was sometimes referred to as the *OKC Spirit*, which was uncommon for most cities and most positive in my view. This assessment, however, was in direct contrast to the plantation mentality others had mentioned in their description of the local culture.

I learned that a hybrid approach would be employed for the staff assigned to the new office. Rather than taking directions solely from D.C. headquarters, this hybrid approach would involve 60% of my direction coming from Washington, 20% from OKC, 10% from Tulsa, and 10% from the regional office in Dallas, Texas. I did not question this approach, but I did wonder how I might satisfy four different offices and bosses.

The temporary office was in a downtown office building on the sixth floor. Two survivors of the bombing were available to me. Later, a government shutdown occurred, and I was instructed to send my two people home during the duration of this uncommon shutdown.

David Long

The Task at Hand

I was advised that I should prepare year-end reports for both the St. Louis office, as well as, for my new office in OKC. I ensured that I had met or exceeded all of the performance goals for the St. Louis office before I left. With the state of affairs being what they were, it would be easy to satisfy this reporting requirement, and I was the only field director responsible for two different field offices in two different regions. After the submission of the reports, I was informed that my performance appraisal was evaluated at just beyond average since I had not yet performed any miracles in OKC. This came from the D.C. supervisor who was not involved in commissioning me to the Oklahoma office.

It was back to the rebuilding processes after the end of the government shutdown. I learned that the regional director wanted to meet with me privately during his first visit to the OKC office. I found a vacant conference room. The regional director quickly informed me that he was there to inform me what my job was, which was to make him look good. He then asked me how I was getting along with the mayor of Tulsa. I told him Susan and I were doing fine. He advised me that I could not call the mayor by her first name. I knew that I had to learn more of the expectations from this regional director.

Shortly after the meeting, I met with the office director at HUD in Tulsa. It was a cordial meeting. He only wanted the same level of attention and programs that I might be able to provide for the city of OKC. Several years later, he invited me to spend a weekend with him at his personal residence in Tulsa at which time he implored me to share how I knew what I knew. Then there was the OKC director who was an officer in the Army Reserve. Considering my own military experience, he said I would know who was in charge and there wouldn't be any problems. I knew what this meant. These officers were the ones I would need to address, along with rebuilding the staff.

As new staff was being hired and brought in, I decided to complain about the memorial headstone that was at the entrance to the HUD office. I mentioned in a staff meeting that I was uncomfortable with this daily reminder. Of course, this observation was not well received by the other staffers, including the office director.

It appeared, to them, that my comments were callous and insensitive to those who were impacted by the bombing. I elected not to yield to these concerns and determined to relocate my office and staff to a different floor. After this was done, a quiet room for reflections was established for the memorial headstone, and this concern was eliminated.

Next, I began to execute a plan that entailed the blending of new employees with the existing two survivors and providing a fresh orientation of how I wanted things done. This process entailed an assessment of prior experiences, training of each staff member, and construction of an individual development plan that included training via vocational/technical support schools, if applicable. Also, my internal training added a different orientation wherein trainees' roles extended beyond the sentry role of federal resources to a role of advancing the department's agenda by using technical assistance provided by the staff to increase the capacity of the recipients. This would become a part of the provider's evaluation.

As word of my enrichment program got around the office, other HUD employees expressed interest in working for me. It could be mentioned that I included myself in training processes by taking several computer courses and a hospitality course at Metro-Tech. Upon completion, I learned that I tested out with the highest score ever recorded for this particular class. My approach also included approved leave for courses during regular work hours and additional consideration for classes at night. In less than a year, the staff was able to provide full servicing to their clients.

There was a wide range of personnel accommodations accorded many of the impacted staff, including the provision of counselors brought in to address the needs of surviving staff. I objected to the notion that the needs of the survivors surpassed and exceeded the needs of the balance of the staff. I rejected the novel accommodation notions and quickly informed my staff that I was there for the resurrection of the office as opposed to a perpetual grieving process. In my world, work was therapy. I reminded my staff that it was my job to see that they did their job, and they should not assume that I would not do *my* job. The easiest way to get along with me would involve them working when they came to work. If you did not feel well, you should take sick leave and stay at home. I was sure the staff got my message.

The following poem reflects my view of the significance and importance of *work*.

WORK–
The Silent Partner

If you are poor
– WORK–
If you are rich, continue to
– WORK–
If you are burdened with seemingly unfair responsibilities
– WORK–
If you are happy, keep right on
– WORKING–
Idleness gives room for doubts and fears.
If disappointments come
– WORK –
If sorrow threatens you
and loved ones seem not true
–WORK–
If health is threatened
– WORK–
When faith falters
and reason fails – just
– WORK–
When dreams are shattered
and hope seems dead
–WORK–
Work as if your life were in peril.
Whatever happens or matters
– WORK –
Work faithfully
Work with faith

Work is the greatest material remedy available.
Work will cure both mental and physical afflictions.

Re-staffing efforts did not go as smoothly as they could have. An uncommon rebidding of a job vacancy was accorded my senior surviving staffer – seemingly on the basis he was impacted by the bombings. The staffer filed an age discrimination suit when he was not selected for the position. I also noted the absence of any minority candidates for the vacancies I was attempting to fill, as per the recommendations from the personnel office located in Fort Worth. Consequently, I undertook my own recruiting process. At the same time, I was required to provide a written explanation of each candidate that I had rejected. It was my misunderstanding that the office's overall staffing would be representative of the composite population where the office was located, if at all practicable.

Additionally, I was aware that I was one of only two Black males presently within the entire office. Although there were several minority females on staff, these numbers did not equate to the 16% minority population. Undeterred, I continued to pursue my action plan.

I quickly determined that it was time for me to separate myself from the other Black male in the office when my housemate advised that should we be trapped in an alley, confronted by hostile parties, and although being back to back to ward off their opponents' parties, that, he, the housemate, said he would not protect my back. I knew it was time to leave.

Another curious spectacle I recall involved a police chase of an inappropriately commandeered beer truck. The truck was being pursued by approximately ten police cars. The truck was halted due to its contact with a downtown office building. The chasing officers surrounded the truck and a canine officer involved in the chase, left the window of the car open just enough for the canine to get out and join in the chase. Unfortunately, it appeared the canine mistook the one Black policeman involved in the chase for the person who had commandeered the truck. The Black officer had to shoot the well-trained canine when it persisted in his chase.

I watched the dog's owner and the shooting officer consoling one another. Several days later, I noticed an "Honors" funeral had been planned for the departed canine.

In light of those factors and influences, I appealed to officials at headquarters (HQ) who candidly advised me of my reputation as a problem solver and my innate ability to quench fires. I was advised that the reality of my situation rested with the view that if I could put out fires then I also had the ability to start one. There was the appearance that even the department was threatened by this gift, and consequently I would have to resolve the problems myself. That also meant that I had to be watched. This assignment was accorded to the OKC manager who relished the opportunity.

I was further reminded of the typical bureaucratic strategies: 1) Blame the victim, 2) List the strengths of the individual as liabilities, and 3) The danger of truth telling versus accepting the party line and the possibility that the victim would not throw himself under the bus for the good of the "Order."

In my view, it was ok to be merely a pawn on someone else's chessboard, but I would not sacrifice my personal integrity.

I got busy and revisited my toolbox in light of the realities as referenced, the decimation of the previous office, and the loss of all records. I had elected to restore the files by asking all grant recipients to forward copies of any HUD correspondence they received over the past five years. I was also aware of a long-standing audit issue with the City of Tulsa in excess of three million dollars. I conceived a plan to resolve this issue and was shortly penalized for doing so.

I was advised that I only mentioned it to the Tulsa office but failed to inform the Washington office, the regional office, and the OKC office in advance of my plan or what it consisted of in regard to the closure of the audit finding. This reprimand did not include the return of the cash prize I won in a golf tourney as part of a statewide conference I attended, and where I discreetly negotiated the resolution of the dated audit finding.

I was also advised that all non-supervisory staff would be accorded the opportunity to work flex hours (anytime between 6AM – 6PM) and that the directors would be required to validate the employees' time. I did not like the prospect of being in the office from six to six. It could be noted that no supervisors were permitted to take advantage of the new flex hour opportunity.

I further recognized that full staffing promise had not been realized. I did not have a deputy/assistant director or program manager. The open secretarial position had not been advertised nor filled. Yet, I had to compensate for these shortages.

After I, and other Black HUD staffers, supported a Black history event in Tulsa that featured a speaker from the Washington D.C. office, I received a travel notice wherein even if no federal travel dollars were involved, and although I would be travelling on my own time (outside normal working hours), advance permission had to be secured from the regional office prior to such travel.

While attending an annual HUD conference (9/11/01) in Arlington, Virginia, breaking news revealed that a plane had crashed into the New York World Trade Center. It was me who advised my New York counterpart that there was a problem. Little did I know of the horrific nature and resulting impacts that would follow.

Shortly thereafter, management staff of the OKC office was summoned to the national office. The secretary for HUD diplomatically explained that the event in New York had resulted in reordering of priorities. Further, the OKC office would receive less attention in OKC's recovery process. I was asked to continue forwarding monthly reports regarding office progress but then shortly after, I was informed that I no longer needed to do that.

I recognized the realities confronting the department and was reminded of a memorial regarding the OKC bombing being established in the courtyard of HUD's national office. I was also aware of OKC's plans for a new federal office building and to establish a national memorial.

I was invited to participate in an executive seminar in Chicago involving several Chicago-based colleges. This leadership development initiative focused on skill developments in a changing environment. I noted, however that one of the instructors had informed the participants of his exposure to the country of Japan and he could speak their language fluently.

At the break, I casually spoke to the instructor in Japanese. I realized that the instructor had overstated his capabilities. Nonetheless, my presence was noted by all in attendance due to my contributions. However, at the end of the conference, I was not mentioned as one of the participants to be selected for promotion to the next grade level.

I, nonchalantly, processed this information and was advised that one of the instructors wanted to visit me since he was originally from OKC. At a subsequent visitation by the instructor, I learned that in spite of my expertise and contributions as a participant at the seminar, a HUD representative had advised the college staff that the national office felt I was in the perfect position to continue to support the department's agenda in OKC. Therefore, I would not be promoted, in spite of the challenges I addressed in an admirable manner.

I knew it was time for another re-assessment as part of my master plan that entailed taking stock of my circumstance 1) to reexamine the environment I was in via my academic training, 2) understand the obstacles via my military training, and 3) develop a survival strategy consistent with my beliefs. This process included the reality that my office phone appeared to be tapped and the reality that my superiors were comfortable with where I was in the system— underscored by their actions. This included the reality that my office would only be accorded the least in terms of staff capacity.

My gift was the deity that my younger brother, Larry Darnell, referenced. This was the person that I had come to know. It was HIM and my assigned Guardian Angel who I had learned to rely upon and it was HIM that I knew I could depend on to guide my footsteps. I knew what I needed to do, and was satisfied that my actions would be covered. While there was little that I knew, I knew where to put my trust. This was the secret weapon I never revealed to those who wanted to know who I knew.

The Chase Goes On

I turned my attention to evolving plans associated with the construction of the new federal building. Countless meetings ensued that would result in a fortress-like building deemed to be the safest and most secure building in the state of Oklahoma. Of course, the general public wouldn't be privy to all the security measures undertaken, wherein the new building was expected to withstand a future bomb.

The staff was relocated to its new facility, diagonally across the national memorial in the downtown area. Several federal agencies, ATF and Social Security were not invited to occupy the new facility as their presence might serve as temptations for future hostile visitations. There were no longer provisions for a daycare center. These determinations were just a few of the planning considerations.

In the new federal building, my staff and I would now be located on the same floor with other HUD staffers. My next door neighbor was the Director of Native American Indians Program. I was to be given a windowless office space similar to the vault I occupied in my hometown. Of course, this is the area where you kept your prized possessions.

Subsequently, I was written up for not following standard practice regarding the location of office files—which would permit anyone to easily access the records germane to the division. Oh well.

I received a call from HQ advising me that an HBCU (Langston) application had been received from my jurisdiction and appeared to be fundable. They inquired if any technical assistance may have been provided since all earlier submissions had been deficient. I acknowledged that I had provided some advice and guidance. I then was informed that I may have violated an *unwritten* rule concerning the provision of TA (technical assistance). I was reminded that this rule *discouraged and prohibited the provision of technical assistance on the basis that one must possess the staffing capacity for all potential applicants as opposed to providing assistance to only one at the exclusion of other potential applicants.*

I assured the caller that would not be a concern because there was only one HBCU in my jurisdiction. I subsequently called the HBCU representative and learned that they had received a call from HQ and excitedly indicated that it was perhaps due to my personal assistance that enabled them to forward a fundable application.

Aha! I said to myself. I was back on my right track. The college president held a press conference and announced the grant. He informed me that now that they had found me, we would be like conjoined twins, joined at the hip forever.

In my view, other notable projects included the restoration of Skirvin Hotel; Citizen's Bank building that featured a gold dome; Sierra Padre Housing Project undertaken by a Mexican builder and resulted in thirty-two residential units being constructed (within a 90 day time period) and was designated as a Best Practice by

DHUD. Further, I presented a check approximating 30 million dollars to the State of Oklahoma in support of its Neighborhood Stabilization Initiatives, which they were reluctant to acknowledge publicly through the news media. It appeared they did not want the public to know they were accepting resources from the Obama Administration. I was told by my HQ superiors to advise the locals that it was the expectation that Obama would be the president of all the states.

At the end of the day, I had reached a point wherein it has been suggested as follows: We have been asked to do so much with so little and for so long that we can now do everything with nothing. When the Obama Administration determined to bail out Wall Street with no relief being accorded to Main Street, I knew it was time for me to leave.

Final OKC Reflections

Upon further introspection, I could be reminded that I influenced decision makers to acknowledge the value of its employees. I was also able to influence the decision makers to incorporate other projects on a nationwide basis vis-à-vis "Best Practices." Nevertheless, I made a mistake when I received my annual performance assessment. It was the assessment for the director in the Alaska office. I felt this was a minor mailing error so I returned it to my boss in D.C. I did not know this would be viewed as a personal affront by my boss and warranted punitive actions against me. The actions included withholding my assessment until the cycle of awards had ended, which meant I wouldn't receive any consideration at all for the fiscal year.

Undeterred, I was pleasantly surprised when my boss's replacement in HQ quietly invited me to share with him how I managed to succeed despite the generally known limited resources accorded me. I confessed that I had rejected the leadership style that featured a top down approach expressed as "my way or the highway." I explained that I favored the *Servant Leadership Model* which suggests that the leader place emphasis on servicing the needs of his subordinate employees and work vigorously to give them the knowledge, skill enrichment training, and resources they need to perform their job.

My new boss accepted my recommendation. It was featured in a subsequent national annual director's meeting with an accompanying book reflecting this management technique. It would be treated as an option to the other traditional management practices and not issued as a requirement.

I felt I had managed to present my gift to others. While unable to unilaterally change the culture of the agency, I was satisfied with my resignation notice that was submitted in 2010. Now for some golf...a game intended to forever keep you humble. At the end of the day, I believe working for the government and being a civil servant is a worthwhile, if not noble profession.

Over the years of my tenure with the Department of Housing and Urban Development, I developed my own personal Hall of Fame. It includes Ted Robinson, Woodrin Key, Cassandra Verret, Sam Riley, Vic Thornton and Ray Willis who were assigned to the Chicago office; William Anderson and Trolius (TC) Warren assigned to the Kansas City office; C. Donald Babers assigned to the Fort Worth office; Steve Bollinger, Terry Duvernay, Patricia Harris and Audrey Prout-Jones assigned to HQ or the Washington office; Sherman Brazil, Joseph (Joe) Baccus and Walter Eschbach stood out in the St. Louis office; and Trina Tollett in the OKC office.

These persons, in my view, met the highest civil service performance standards and served in a meritorious and exemplary manner, which encouraged me to be the best that I could be.

♣

In spite of the impediments I was exposed to and challenged by, I never revealed all I knew. I always resisted, and never accepted, the notion that I was a rival or an adversarial threat to my peers, boss, or the executive I reported to. At the end of the day, I confessed that there may have been a little jealously in the mix, but that was the little that I knew which guided and undergirded my successful journey and career. Of course, the little that I knew accepted the reality that my G.A. seemingly was always at my side and in my corner. That is the one that can be commended.

One of the best compliments I was accorded was related to the OKC's office manager at a special emphasis program who deviated from the scripted agenda by failing/refusing to introduce me as Master of Ceremonies for the event.

Finally, my present gift is to, and for, those persons who wanted me to tell them who I knew. My response/gift is that I can't recall when the realization came to me that I am not only my daddy's son but my Father's son also.

My Inheritance

Parents are funny. Most tried to tell you stuff. Oftentimes it would be stuff that appeared to be confusing and even stuff we did not want to hear. Many parents worked hard from sunrise to sunset, at teaching, training, nourishing, mentoring, and basically trying to show us the way. They routinely pointed out the right from the wrong. They told us that the long way home was usually the best way home. Few, however could explain or took the time to tell us how they came to know what they knew. We never really asked the question but it was clear that they felt it was their responsibility to try to prepare us for the realities of a hostile world.

They did what they could, based upon the lessons that life taught them. Many were not permitted to finish grade school and were typically assigned to the class of *you can't* or *you better not*. They taught us the alphabet, and while we didn't have much of it, we learned how to count money. We struggled with the pronouncement that the nearest helping hands ought to be found at the end of our own arms and many other parabolic stories. We mastered the art of making lemonade, digesting humble pie, and how to straighten up and fly right. We played games like marbles, hopscotch, and horses, along with hide and go seek.

When I was about to leave the nest, my dad (man of few words) told me to look for a good woman. His words and actions now appear to be reflected in several songs, addressing the notion of RESPECT. Even the fellas at the neighborhood watering hole advised that beauty was only skin deep, but ugliness could be found to the bone. I'm also not sure if everyone figured out exactly who was the member of the opposite sex.

I am reminded that the man of few words opined that there were only two kinds of knowledge: *what you know* and *what you don't know*. He trusted that you had enough sense to obtain that which you didn't know from those who did know. Your ego or your desire to fly by the seat of your pants should be ignored in this regard.

Parents generally tried to encourage, I believe, their children. They wanted us to be somebody they could be proud of, someone they could claim as their own. I remember my dad claiming me when I accidentally backed the truck into our barbecue grill. I heard him say, "Yes, that's my son." On another occasion, when I failed to make the high school football team, he had me to know that I was still his son. I could mention that on other occasions he advised that a man's name was most important. You could gleam some insights just from examining a man's name. Often, people became known for one thing or another. This reference, in the main, defined them and indeed became their reputation.

Communication was another tricky area. There were some things they did not want us to know. There were other things we came to know because we figured them out. They were pleased with our progress leading to understanding. I believe some of this communication was done or not done to somehow protect us. Many of our questions were treated with grandmotherly *hums* and *you don't say*. Of course, *umph umph umph* was most telling.

One of my uncles advised my dad that he felt I had some potential and quite a bit of wit. My dad acknowledged the potential but felt that he was only half right about my wit. Consequently, I was surprised, after high school graduation, he advised that I should consider becoming a doctor while underscoring that he had absolutely no resources he could make available to this end. The military became one of a few limited options for me.

Regarding my return from boot camp, my parents informed me they would be waiting for me at the train station. I can still hear my dad's excitement when he saw me and shouted, "Boy, am I glad to see you. When are you leaving?"

I must confess that I don't know what your parents may have told you. I do believe that you might have been gazed upon in wonderment and through loving eyes. If the eyes could have talked, they would have told you of the hopes, dreams, and the many good wishes they held for you. Those same eyes, I believe, would have tried to shield some of the outstanding challenges that they struggled with on a daily basis. The harsh realities of discrimination, second class citizenship, and racism, just to mention some of the trials and tribulations certain parents and grandparents came to know all too well.

I can also admit that other younger voices appear to be confused. It makes me wonder what they were told and not told. For example, I innocently asked a young man (who appeared to be a spry teenager and was reclining against a large tree) if he would tell me what the term *freedom* meant. Without hesitancy, he indicated that freedom meant the opportunity to do absolutely nothing and he was resting because he heard that his grandparents were slaves. So he was taking the rest they did not receive.

You may have heard that acorns don't fall that far away from the tree. You may have also heard people say, "the baby does have his father's nose or his lips" or "fortunately she took after her mother." Then, there is the story of the chicken and the duck. Do we talk enough about where diamonds come from? Some call it coal, others carbon, which is subjected to uncommon pressure as well as heat to be transformed into one of the most expensive gems on the planet earth.

In acknowledgement of the real parents' and grandparents' contribution, it is my understanding that because of what they did, and in many instances what they didn't do, we know in our hearts and now in our minds what it is we ought to be doing. The correct decision is not hidden from us. We don't need our best social friends to tell us what we should be doing. Let's be real for a moment—the temptations are always ready, willing and able, but our minds make us stronger and capable of resisting these impulses. Energy and effort seldom have time for careless and lazy, much less pure and foolishness.

We have all heard it: *I don't want to get involved. Let someone else do it.* We continue to witness all kinds of deflections and deceptions. However, at the end of the day, it might be interesting to know just how many believe that they have completely severed all ties to their DNA.

The mysteries and vagaries of our DNA are yet being studied. There remain untold chapters and unfinished publications on this subject. Yet, we know in terms of geography, from whence we have come, but beyond the misery of that journey few can tell of the triumphs over tragedy, the innovativeness and ingenuity, the coping and leadership skills, and indeed the richness and magnificence that is traceable through our lineage. This is in spite of the disconnections that have occurred beyond our control.

Knowing who you are, valuing the uniqueness of self, and recognizing that the better place to initiate love begins with us to the extent that we understand that it is permissible for us to care for ourselves. These notions and principles were part of the foundations that our parents inherently attempted to convey to us in so many ways. Preparation is, in many instances, still searching for chance and opportunity. Being anointed does not guarantee certain appointments. Our goal and vision has not diminished in terms of the simple challenge to be the best that we can be.

While I wanted to believe that our parents gave us little to nothing, I have now concluded that they gave us everything. They gave us life. They gave us love. Our inheritance embraces and includes the values, principles, and standards of excellence that we could not see at the time. How could I choose material things over their uncommon sacrifices and the wisdom of their insights. The correct answer is...I wouldn't.

About the Author

"I don't view my civil service career as a complete failure, in spite of my best efforts to eliminate poverty, shelter the homeless, and provide decent and safe housing for those persons within my jurisdictions." Long's academic background includes a Bachelor of Science and a MBA (1974) from Southern Illinois University at Edwardsville, Illinois. He initially worked in the housing field before serving as an urban planner and local administrator of federal funds for the city of East St. Louis. His past and present affiliations include memberships with the Urban League, American Society of Public Administrators, and the Masonic Order where he achieved the status of a 32nd degree Mason.

Long served as the director/mentor for the John H. Johnson Boys' Club in East St. Louis, has been cited by Marquis Who's Who, Inc., is a former officer of the National Community Development Directors Association, and held membership with the International Optimist Club. He served as the Secretary for the Board of Trustees at his former church and served as a co-chairman of a successful $750,000 building fund program that resulted in the construction of a new sanctuary for Prospect Missionary Baptist Church in Oklahoma City under the leadership of Dr. Lee E. Cooper.

Long served two terms as president of Eastern Golf Club. After 15 years, he retired as the director of their junior golf program, which provides free golf lessons and scholarships on an annual basis to area youth.

Since Long's retirement, he proudly boasts that his wife, Ermentine, a retired nurse, has first claim and priority with him. He is confident retirement will work itself out.

Long is the father of two adult daughters and one adult son. He is the proud grandfather to several grandchildren, including Xavier Woods, a WWE professional wrestler. This is Long's first published literary work.

To contact this author to arrange speaking engagements or to purchase copies of this book please email the author at:

David Long
onedelong123@yahoo.com

Made in the USA
Monee, IL
12 June 2021

71045737R10079